Wedding Readings

Also by Eleanor Munro

THROUGH THE VERMILION GATES

ORIGINALS: AMERICAN WOMEN ARTISTS

ON GLORY ROADS: A PILGRIM'S BOOK ABOUT PILGRIMAGE

MEMOIR OF A MODERNIST'S DAUGHTER

Wedding Readings

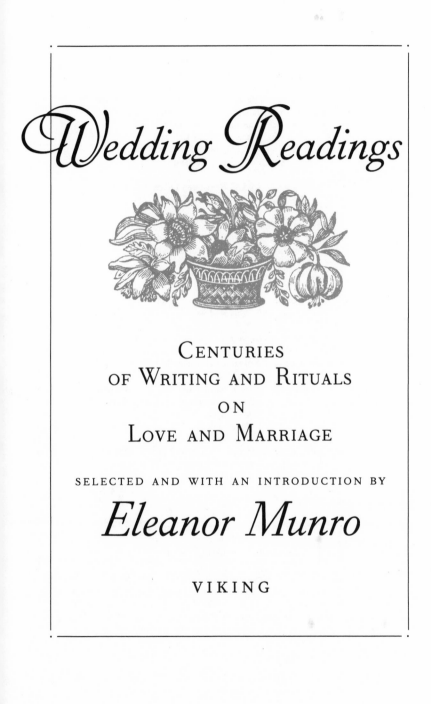

CENTURIES
OF WRITING AND RITUALS
ON
LOVE AND MARRIAGE

SELECTED AND WITH AN INTRODUCTION BY

Eleanor Munro

VIKING

VIKING
Published by the Penguin Group
Viking Penguin, a division of Penguin Books USA Inc.,
40 West 23rd Street, New York, New York 10010, U.S.A.
Penguin Books Ltd, 27 Wrights Lane, London W8 5TZ, England
Penguin Books Australia Ltd, Ringwood, Victoria, Australia
Penguin Books Canada Ltd, 2801 John Street,
Markham, Ontario, Canada L3R 1B4
Penguin Books (N.Z.) Ltd, 182–190 Wairau Road,
Auckland 10, New Zealand

Penguin Books Ltd, Registered Offices:
Harmondsworth, Middlesex, England

First published in 1989 by Viking Penguin,
a division of Penguin Books USA Inc.
Published simultaneously in Canada

1 3 5 7 9 10 8 6 4 2

An extension of this copyright page begins on page 259.

LIBRARY OF CONGRESS CATALOGING IN PUBLICATION DATA
Munro, Eleanor C.
Wedding readings : centuries of writing and rituals on love and
marriage / selected and with an introduction by Eleanor Munro.
p.   cm.
Includes index.
ISBN 0-670-81088-6
1. Weddings—Literary collections.   2. Love—Literary collections.
3. Marriage—Literary collections.   I. Title.
PN6071.W4M86   1989
082—dc19   88-40334
                                                                              CIP

Printed in the United States of America
Set in Fournier
Designed by Francesca Belanger

For David and Anath

August 28, 1988

Acknowledgments

Nan Graham of Viking inspired this book. She recognized the need for such a resource. She understood that many couples approaching marriage today want to formalize their hopes within the embrace of ritual both old and modern, traditional and also distinctively personal. And because of the course of much of my own writing so far—about imaginative people's lives and their quest or pilgrimage toward form and meaning in them—she thought I'd find the idea interesting. She was right on both scores. Many people spoke to me about their search for appropriate additions to liturgies of their choice, and a number of clergymen and women did as well. As for me, as I worked my way through the library, I became more and more impressed by the delicacy of their—and my—mission.

The artifices of courtship have changed radically in the past century, but the achievement of a good marriage hasn't been made easier by these upheavals. The challenge for people marrying today is to know what they want from the institution. If their view of it is serious, as most people's is, they'll want to spend time thinking hard about that question. It seems to me that to do so helped along by others from far-flung parts of the world and many past centuries, who've ruminated on the same issues of love, hope, permanence, and related subjects, can't help but be illuminating.

In spite of all that in these days separates us from the language and customs of our forebears, still, as Keats wrote, "some shape of beauty" moves us toward salvaging the essentials in the old ceremonies like those of marriage. The question that confronts people approaching marriage today, then, is: what are the essentials? That question lies at the heart of the contents and organization of this book.

Many poems and prose passages appear in these pages in excerpted form. I owe an explanation of my use of that editorial privilege. In my days as an editor of an art magazine, I learned the effectiveness of details of larger works isolated on a page. At the same time, we understood that to highlight a detail was to do a kind of violence to the complete work, and we always included a small photo of the whole work as a reference. Looking for literary selections appropriate to marriage, I found myself under a constraint. Much writing on love draws power from the dialectic at the heart of human life: the longing for permanence and the absoluteness of passing time. But the marriage ritual, theoretically a timeless sacrament, opposes the literalness of decay. Soundings of realism which give weight to a poem on the page would be horribly inappropriate to the mood of a wedding. So in full if abashed awareness, I offer the light from many of these works without the necessary, more truthful dark. It would have been good to print such poems in full as well, as we used to do with paintings. But the whole works can be found in many places, and I trust readers, once the wedding day is past, to draw on their collective wisdom.

In addition to Nan Graham, others helped shape this book. Graphic designer Francesca Belanger gave it its visual clarity. Ann Bartunek was its expert copy editor. Kate Griggs and Kathryn Harrison, also of Viking, were patient and careful through its changes. For leads, encouragement and other helps, I also thank Georges and Anne Borchardt, Lynn Boillot, Caryn Beth Broitman, William Rossa Cole, the Reverend Jean Curtis, Helen

Handley, Francine Klagsbrun, Stanley Kunitz, the Reverend and Mrs. Edward L. Mark, Pamela Painter, Dawn E. Rickman, Jeannette Rohatyn, David and Catherine Shainberg, Maggie Scarf, Eileen Simpson, William Jay Smith, Carol Southern, the Reverend James E. Thomas, Aileen Ward, Mark Williams, Nancy Dingman Watson, and Peter and Clara Watson.

Thanks too to my extended family—now eight nuclear families and more no doubt on the horizon—who have taught me much about love and forbearance, the twin supports of the married life.

Contents

I. *The Time Is Come*

II. *In Search of Love*

III. *The Processional Begins*

IV. *Eternal Vows in Sacred Space*

V. *The Miracle of the Body*

VI. *The Country of Marriage*

Wedding Readings

. . . our life reminds me
of a forest in which there is a graceful clearing
and in that opening a house,
an orchard and garden,
comfortable shades, and flowers . . .
The forest is mostly dark, its ways
to be made anew day after day, the dark
richer than the light and more blessed,
provided we stay brave
enough to keep on going in . . .

WENDELL BERRY, from "The Country of Marriage"

Apparently I am going to marry Charles Lindbergh. . . . Don't
wish me happiness—it's gotten beyond that, somehow. Wish
me courage and strength and a sense of humor—I will need
them all. . . .

ANNE MORROW LINDBERGH, from *Bring Me a Unicorn*

. . . when we find ourselves
In the place just right
It will be in the valley
Of love and delight.

from "Simple Gifts,"
a Shaker hymn

The he country of marriage, in *Wendell Berry's* lovely phrase, lies well beyond careless happiness, on the other side of but never out of reach of the valley of delight. A person can drop straight into the place as if by parachute, but the long winding and climbing approach is more interesting. In either case, once there, you have a lot to learn. But when the harvests roll in, they're full and mellow. Each day then breaks like a birthing—no other has been so fresh and new. And night, when it comes, comes easy. Moonlight veils the houses and fields; stars rise, flare, pale, and disappear—to return the next night as if the world had no end.

The ritual which is the gateway into this country or condition is the wedding. In the present day, a wedding has two functions. One is to confirm the bridal couple in their own religious or social heritage against the larger background of cultural history. The other is to address the pair as individuals, leading each one toward an understanding of what it can mean to exchange vows of fidelity and care in this age of radical self-questioning and social change. The ceremony at the gate is one of the "rites of passage," as anthropologists call them, by which people in different parts of the world signal their entry into a new stage of life.

To the wedding formalities, the readings in this book provide a sort of counterpoint. Some of the meditations on the nature of love and union would probably best be read by a couple in private, separately or together. Others should fit gracefully into the proceedings of even the most traditional wedding. Personal additions to the liturgy are allowed today by most Jewish and Christian clergy, who will guide couples in making their choices of readings, assigning them to family members or close friends, and setting them in the proper place in the ceremony.

Included here are passages of scripture and liturgy from various parts of the world, including India and China, as well as secular literature old and new, some of which, in the words of the poet Wallace Stevens, address "the men of the time . . . and the women of the time." In their various voices these writers have sought to describe a mode of feeling which had its origin in our common animal need for protection, warmth, and companionship, but which has evolved over the centuries into something more general and far-reaching. The sensibility these writers have tried to define, which they celebrate and toward which we move in hope and trust as we approach marriage, is experienced as the fundamental orienting principle of a life. In an age of shifting values and emotional inconstancies, of restlessness and faithlessness, the concept of enduring love and the institution which embodies it serves us well.

In a poem about modern poetry, Wallace Stevens makes his way slowly, even gropingly, toward an idea which is only just coming into his mind as he proceeds. "It has to be living," he says, "to learn the/speech of the place.

> . . . [to] speak words that in the ear,
> In the delicatest ear of the mind, repeat,
> Exactly, that which it wants to hear, at the sound
> Of which, an invisible audience listens,
> Not to the play, but to itself, expressed
> In an emotion as of two people, as of two
> Emotions becoming one. . . .

Both the art of modern poetry, as Stevens understands it, and the art of modern marriage entail moving persistently but perhaps not ever quite successfully toward an ideal held in the mind. For a modern person to prepare for marriage in that sense may mean acquiring an understanding of the ideal which will be sturdy enough to survive one's continued failure to achieve it.

The concept of Love as an abstract ideal is credited to the Greek philosopher Plato. Much of the world's literature on romantic and mystical love, including the Jewish and Christian marriage liturgies, take their tone from that source. Perfect Love is a god, Plato proposed, divine, everlasting, and as unattainable by human beings as the stars. In that form, Love has existed in the universe since the beginning of time and will endure forever. On the other hand, there exists also the individual brand of love, which strikes us here on earth like a glint off the sun, making us suffer, pine, rejoice, and, sometimes, marry.

As Plato saw it, the most important thing about Love in the general sense was its power to draw people toward it, to stir in them "a longing for immortality, which in the human consciousness begins with a desire for union." We still don't fully understand what "desire for union" means in terms of human psychology. Perhaps it begins in adolescence with a feeling of nostalgia for the security of infancy. But whenever in later life it surges back, it moves people young and old, in their individual times of readiness, toward marriage or some comparable state of emotional bonding.

The ritual forms by which marriage is inaugurated, those liturgies and the formal postures and actions of the participants, take some of their tone of solemn otherworldliness from Platonic thought as well. These rites come down to us as if out of the clouds, seemingly without connection to everyday language and behavior. In the same way, family histories, often recalled in toasts during wedding festivities, transcend ordinary time. Such summonings of ancestral lines link up the centuries through repeated rhythms of marriage, birth, and death, the "periods of return" of humanity's adventure under the stars. Wound around by these formulations while a wedding unfolds, an individual may feel very small or very important but never alone. The ceremonies, and reminders of long family participation in them, serve to draw young people two by two into the ark of our common heritage. Say the ancient words and you join the generations to live a larger life than your own.

In this sense, marriage is a form of thought and imagination. It is a structure laid around the fruitful period of a lifetime within which otherwise random experiences and years acquire purpose and shape. In that enclosure—in that country—love is twined with the notion of timelessness; awakened sexuality, with trust. The importance in the evolution of human thinking of this double helix of love and timelessness is suggested by the reverence people still feel for the capacity of lifelong fidelity to an ideal or person. The biblical promise "Whither thou goest, I will go . . ." is a pledge which gave the Moabite woman Ruth new awareness of both place and time, for before the promise was made, neither nation nor years had special significance for her, nor had her life a special end. But giving up her homeland to serve her husband's mother, she won respect and love, and a place in the noblest family tree in Western scripture, that of King David. To make a pledge of perpetual loyalty, of the kind marriage entails, is still to lend oneself to the long human quest for moral value.

In antiquity in both Asia and the pagan West, myths of stable (or unstable) bonds between the various gods served as a metaphor for the relationship between elements of the natural world. Sky gods in wedlock with goddesses of the earth, field gods in seasonal marriage with corn and wheat goddesses, represented the enduring if periodically unsettled universe. In ancient Rome, a human male sometimes took on the mantle of a god and was wed to a tree in Diana's sacred grove in the Alban hills, where she reigned as goddess of woodlands and wild animals. Today we accept that that rite symbolized the bond between humanity and the world, on which the continued well-being of each depends. Projecting the image of a marriage bond onto nature, men and women in antiquity humanized the earth at the same time that they magnified their sense of their own place in creation.

The myth of wedlock with the natural world did not pass away. It survives today openly in the wedding rites of Hinduism, a religious community which extends across India, parts of Indonesia and Africa, and into smaller pockets in the West. Bridegroom and bride represent Lord Shiva, creator and destroyer of the world, and his wife, Parvati. They also represent Lord Shiva's shrine-city Benares in India, which is understood to be in perpetual nuptial union with the goddess Ganga, the river Ganges, which flows along its bank. Beyond that, they represent the halves of the cosmos itself: "I am the sky," says the bridegroom to his bride as part of the ritual. "You are the earth. We are sky and earth, united." At the close of their wedding day, the couple stands together under the stars while the husband points out the constellations as they rise, ending with the North Star, to which he makes a ritual prayer:

O Firm one, pillar of the stars, Polestar, how stable you are! As the earth is stable, as the mountains are stable, as the universe is stable, so may this woman my wife be firm and stable in our family.

Then he turns to his wife: "You are united with me. May you live with me for a hundred years! May you be steadfast as that star in your love for me." She acquiesces with the promise to be "ever firmly attached to my husband." Thereafter, husband and wife are each the other's Polestar, and so it may be for married couples wherever they are, whatever their religious orientation.

In the city of Venice for many centuries a comparable rite was performed. The magistrate of the city, the Doge, took on himself the role of bridegroom, throwing a gold ring into the waves of the Adriatic with the words, Desponsamus te, Mare . . . : *We wed thee, O Sea. The rest of the liturgy informed the bride of her perpetual domination by the Venetian Republic. Now that city is no more a political power in itself, and in the West at least the old concept of divinely appointed male authority has faded, but the power of the ritual remains, for it* contained psychological truth. It speaks to us today. It tells us to make our lives a union of structure and emotion. It reminds us that social forms like marriage are drawn out of the universal human well-source of need and desire.

Enduring loyalty is one such structure, which stands like a Venice on the shores of the aimlessness and emptiness which for many people characterize life without it. "I do love thee," said Shakespeare's Othello. "And when I love thee not/Chaos is come again." It is against chaos that many modern writers represented in these pages, like E. M. Forster, W. H. Auden, Wallace Stevens, and others, some of whom were in fact unmarried, others whose marriages were less than satisfying, still described the institution as precious and good.

The symbolism of divine marriage with its apparatus of incantation and magic is still with us. Wedding vows in that sense are spells, invocations not so much to heaven as to a still-unrealized being in oneself who may grow to maturity to fulfill the promise. Often when a wedding takes place in a public place, a small crowd gathers on the sidewalk to wait for the bride. When she comes out the door to stand at the top of the steps, in her white dress with her white veil turned back, she seems more than herself, even a little like a goddess. We are all prone to the illusion. We believe, or want to believe, that a union of two of ourselves, formalized by a wedding, will in some way outlast our lives. Even unbelievers cast themselves forward in marriage through the hope of children, or if not of children, of some other version of the creative old words, to "husband the earth."

So wedding rites and the associations we have with them, like other rites of passage through history, prove that the human family is one, even if its members are as varied as birds in their mating feathers and songs. Whether we identify ourselves as Jewish, Catholic, or Protestant; Hindu, Buddhist, or Moslem; tribal or atheist, we inherit a disposition felt as a lifelong need to shape our thoughts and lives in symbolic terms against the background of the world. Our rites of passage, their formal *language and stately pantomimes on the theme of union between humanity and the cosmos, are an answer to this need.*

On the other hand, each individual has to find his or her own footing in the ceremony with its architecture of enduring time and moral responsibility. The readings here may provide some guidance. The selections are grouped loosely into sections which follow the narrative course of the event. In the first group are passages by various writers on the theme of psychic change and preparation for a great decision. The next includes meditations on the nature and meaning of love, beginning with Plato's Symposium. *Thereafter come selections on the ceremony itself, on the signifance of the "sacred space" where the vows are exchanged, and passages of liturgy, poetry, and prose on related mysteries.*

According to ancient myths, sacred space is a site where earth and sky meet, as on a holy mountaintop or in a shrine, temple, or church which has been ritually sanctified. There, according to the myths, time stands still. History dissolves into eternity. The implications of this mystical belief reach out to affect bridal couples today. The Jewish or Christian bride and groom represent the biblical Eve and Adam and later scriptural queens and kings. Bridal couples in the Greek and Russian Orthodox churches wear gold crowns for this reason, as do couples in Indonesia, who represent their own royal and religious ancestors.

In sacred space, every detail of ritual flows from the concept of united earth and heaven. As the wedding day approaches, the site where the ceremony is to be held is ritualistically readied. A garden is planted, watered, and nurtured into bloom. A shrine is cleaned and decorated with flowers, and the instruments of the service, Jewish, Catholic, or Protestant, laid out. In Asia, the shrine is purified by burning herbs and holy oils in it and reciting mantras or magic spells. In a Buddhist shrine, an altar table is set with twin vases of flowers or pine branches, together with a bowl of holy water and prayer beads, and perhaps memorial tablets of both families.

On the wedding day, the bridal couple is prepared to enter the symbolic space. Jewish couples, separately, visit the mikvah or holy bath, whose waters, according to tradition, flow out of the Jordan River to wash away the stains of the world. In Asia, the bride and groom may be rubbed in unguents and spices, ground mustard seed or myrtle, and the palms of their hands and the soles of their feet stained with henna. The bride's hair is arranged and adorned with gold ornaments and flowers.

Finally comes the ceremonial dressing. In Asia, bride and groom wear silks and crowns of royalty and colors taken from nature's palette: red or gold of sunlight, blue of heaven, green of grass. In the West, we reserve only the bridegroom's buttonhole for such unpuritan display, and our brides wear white for angelic unworldliness.

When the couple enters the sanctuary, they stand in ritually prescribed formation, for where they stand represents the center of earth and heaven, the pin of a cosmic compass. A Jewish wedding takes place under a chuppah, or canopy, held upon four poles, which represents the sky of paradise. There the bride first takes her position facing the bridegroom as, in Genesis, Eve was presented to Adam. She then moves to his right to receive the wedding ring on the index finger of her right hand, whose artery, it was once thought, was joined to the heart. In Christian sanctuaries, couples stand before the altar which, architectural necessities permitting, faces east toward sunrise, the direction in which according to old tradition Christ rose to heaven. Standing at her bridegroom's left, the Christian bride receives her ring on her left hand, the heart hand of this tradition.

In Judaism and Christianity, human marriage is said to mirror the union of God and humanity. Western wedding liturgies are filled with expressions of mystical love in which the bridegroom's love for his bride reflects God's for men and women. Committing themselves to fidelity beyond the grave in a ceremony which includes celebration of the Eucharist or Mass, Catholic couples assume symbolic roles referring to God's husbanding of his people and Christ's of his church on earth. Protestant weddings may be shy on mystic symbolism but they include an incomparable rhetoric of instruction to the new family on the responsibilities of humanhood. The language in the revised Book of Common Prayer has entered the bloodstream of the English-speaking world: "Dearly beloved: We have come together in the presence of God to witness and bless the joining together of this man and this woman in Holy Matrimony. . . ." In the Eastern Orthodox Church, by contrast, mood and symbolism count heavily. Bride and bridegroom enter the sanctuary carrying lighted white candles, led by robed priests swinging censers. To the sound of prolonged medieval choral singing, they exchange rings in a ritual betrothal, then don gold crowns for the exchange of vows.

The number seven appears in the liturgies of Judaism, Catholicism, and Hinduism. As with other details of marriage ritual, we have to seek the reason in the past where the roots of belief lie tangled with ancient suppositions about the nature of the world. The number refers to the earth, sun, moon, and four planets visible to the naked eye all apparently locked together in harmonious interrelationship governed by a single law. To speak of "seven" then means to speak of a whole, a cosmic union. Jewish weddings include seven ritual blessings. In the Roman Catholic Church, marriage is one of the seven sacraments. And in the course of their wedding, a Hindu bride and groom take seven steps around a stone or fire on the altar representing the axis of the universe while they pray for seven blessings on their future lives. "We have taken the seven steps," says the groom. "You are mine forever."

The vows in these and other ceremonies bind a couple several ways: subjectively in their own consciousness of the new life they are entering; in a social sense into their community, in which the vows may have legal weight; finally into the fabric of immemorial myth and faith, in which the words are believed to lend stabilizing power to the universe itself.

At the same time all these evolved ideas about marriage hide the simple fact of nature which is the basis for the social ceremony: a man and woman's readiness for monogamous sexual life, their acceptance of adult responsibility. When the groom slips a ring on the bride's finger, he takes possession of her, in the language of symbolism, in the flesh. In Jewish tradition, when the bride and bridegroom share red wine from a goblet, they symbolically take in the fruit of each other's love. So of the nuptial kiss at the end of Christian services and the winding of a newly married couple in flower wreaths and ribbons. So of the flinging of rice and the banging of pot lids at the newlyweds' door: all these are not-so-veiled references to sexual union. In some rural communities and intensely mystical religious sects like the Jewish Hasidim, it is usual to celebrate weddings with sexually charged dances around the bridal couple lifted on high chairs at the center. These exercises may come down the ages and distantly imitate the circling of stars around the axis of the earth, the most glorious image of union the world affords.

Mystics may dance, and nature lovers find wider resonance to their lovemaking at Niagara Falls, but for many young people in the world today a wedding is occasion for somber rites of integration into their nations' history. When the Orthodox Jewish bridegroom crushes a glass under his foot at the end of the ceremony, he metaphorically enacts his union with his bride and, at the same time, recalls the tragedy that still overhangs Jewish national life, the destruction of the Temple. And in Russia today, brides still in white after their bureaucratic weddings make pilgrimage with their husbands to historic places like Lenin's tomb in Red Square in Moscow, the Tomb of the Unknown Soldier of the "Great Fatherland War of 1941–45," or, in the provinces, any statue of Lenin. Reverently they lay down their bouquets on the stones, pose for pictures, and uncork champagne to share with passersby. The legend on the base of the Moscow tomb reads "Your name is unknown but your deed is eternal." The notion of eternality in materialist Soviet Russia is a relic from its Christian past, but reverence for the honored dead is common, and by these actions, couples publicly announce their claim on a larger-than-ordinary life. In a rite even more indicative of the deep meaning of the marriage bond, some hundred couples a year travel to the site of the village of Lidice in Czechoslovakia, destroyed by the Nazis, to be married there and so in some sense carry on its life.

However, the word "eternity" may be too remote and abstract to convey the reality of what most marrying couples today hunger for. All these rites and symbolisms of marriage—the cosmic imagery of the Hindu wedding, the crowns worn by Greek Orthodox brides and bridegrooms, the paradisiacal significance of the Jewish chuppah, the biblical resonances of the Western Christian service, even the angelic white worn by brides in many countries—serve to situate the institution against an expanded background of space, time, myth, and history. Modern couples still long for what their forebears provided the symbolic means of experiencing: a living bond with the world which will outlast their lives.

That longing, and the ideas and images it generates, underlie the final group of readings in this collection, which opens with James Agee's meditation on a house in country-morning sunlight. Call that house "marriage." It stands square and solid on the plains, lit by light from beyond the horizon. So of marriage. It is a monumental, grounded structure in our individual lives as in society. It was built to answer a physical need: to provide shelter and nurture for the fragile offspring of our species. But it reflects these other, less tangible needs.

It was once upon a time imagined that mistletoe in the boughs of an oak tree held the juice of immortality, or Love. The plant was said to bloom on Midsummer Eve. A girl would spread a white cloth under the tree that night, take the flower dust found there and sprinkle it under her pillow to see her future bridegroom in her dream. Good luck, lasting marriage, and long life were conjured for in many such ways in the old days. Girls in rural America spent their years of adolescence stitching quilts to the number eleven, when they'd let be known their readiness for a suitor, then set to work on the twelfth, the Wedding Quilt, which would be done in time for the bridal bed.

We're not so easily charmed into faith today. But there may be mysterious benefit to be had from the kind of meditations I've included in the section "Morning in Eternal Space." These readings lift the curtain on what will be, henceforth, for each couple their landscape of marriage. Oriented in the center of it as if by the Blackfoot prayer to the four directions or the Chinese prayer to the four seasons, they may petition the skies for the kind of simple gifts with which true happiness begins—"calm lake, little wind, little rain . . . moon of good health . . . the year abundant, with millet and rice . . ."—the promise of full harvests for years to come.

All that I've said here applies both to committed members of religious communities and to couples embarking on the kind of secular, or inter-faith, and cross-cultural marriages common in our society today. In all these cases both bride and bridegroom will let widen their mental horizons to make space for the new axis of their joined lives. Then the very process of putting together the ceremony can become a ritual of initiation into a life of examined, shared values. Readings and other personal contri-butions by the couple to one another can be like flags planted at the outermost boundaries of their hopes for the future, while those contributed by the elders may contain modicums of the life-tempered wisdom once handed down, parent to child, by the old ones of the tribe.

Or so the elders hope.

I

The Time Is Come

Hippe, the maiden, has put up her abundant curly hair, brushing it from her perfumed temples, for the time when she must marry is come. Now Artemis, in your loving kindness, grant this girl, who has bidden good-bye to her knucklebones, both husband and children.

Timareta, the daughter of Timaretus, before her wedding, has dedicated to you, Artemis of the lake, her tambourine and her pretty ball, and the net that kept up her hair, and her dolls too and their dresses. Hold your hand over the girl, Artemis, to keep her safe.

Ancient Greek dedications to brides

*Y*ou are considering being married or on the way to that point. Or your wedding day is already set and you're thinking about the ceremony, looking for passages of poetry or prose to add to your community's liturgy. In the latter case, you'll already have passed through a process of inner change, readying yourself for a new stage of life. While formal wedding ceremonies lead the participants step by step toward a symbolic rite of full commitment, secular writers have paid more attention to the tentative, even painful steps of psychic preparation for the event. The selections which follow contain the thoughts of various ancient and modern writers on this theme of preparation for a great decision—a counterpoint to the stately, assured procedures of the ceremony itself.

Behold, I have set before you an open door, and no man shall close it.

Revelation 3:8 (New English Bible)

God has dressed me with garments of exultation . . . As a bridegroom puts on a priestly diadem, and as a bride adorns herself with her jewels. For, as the earth puts forth her blossoms or bushes in the garden burst into flower, so shall the Lord God make righteousness and praise blossom before all the nations.

Isaiah 61:10–11 (New English Bible)

. . . I saw emptiness under the sun: a lonely man without a friend, without son or brother, toiling endlessly yet never satisfied with his wealth—"For whom," he asks, "am I toiling and denying myself the good things of life?" This too is emptiness, a sorry business. Two are better than one; they receive a good reward for their toil, because, if one fails, the other can help his companion up again; but alas for the man who falls alone with no partner to help him up. And, if two lie side by side, they keep each other warm; but how can one keep warm by himself? If a man is alone, an assailant may overpower him, but two can resist; and a cord of three strands is not quickly snapped.

Ecclesiastes 4:7–13 (New English Bible)

There be many shapes of mystery,
And many things God makes to be,
    past hope or fear,
And the end men looked for cometh not,
And a path is there where no one sought.
    So hath it fallen here.

EURIPIDES

I got me flowers to straw thy way;
I got me boughs off many a tree:
But thou wast up by break of day,
And brought'st thy sweets along with thee.

The Sunne arising in the East,
Though he give light, & th' East perfume;
If they should offer to contest
With thy arising, they presume.

Can there be any day but this,
Though many sunnes to shine endeavour?
We count three hundred, but we misse:
There is but one, and that one ever.

GEORGE HERBERT, from "Easter"

We're too old to be single. Why shouldn't we both be married instead of sitting through the long winter evenings by our solitary firesides? Why shouldn't we make one fireside of it?

Come, let's be a comfortable couple and take care of each other! How glad we shall be, that we have somebody we are fond of always, to talk to and sit with.

Let's be a comfortable couple. Now do, my dear!

CHARLES DICKENS

You say, to me-wards your affection's strong;
Pray love me little, so you love me long.
Slowly goes farre: The meane is best: Desire
Grown violent, do's either die, or tire.

ROBERT HERRICK, "Love Me Little, Love Me Long"

. . . the future enters into us . . . in order to transform itself in us long before it happens. And this is why it is so important to be lonely and attentive when one is sad: because the apparently uneventful and stark moment at which our future sets foot in us is so much closer to life than that other noisy and fortuitous point of time at which it happens to us as if from outside. The more still, more patient and more open we are when we are sad, so much the deeper and so much the more unswervingly does the new go into us, so much the better do we make it ours, so much the more will it be *our* destiny, and when on some later day it "happens" (that is, steps forth out of us to others), we shall feel in our inmost selves akin and near to it. And that is necessary. It is necessary—and toward this our development will move gradually—that nothing strange should befall us, but only that which has long belonged to us. We have . . . to realize that that which we call destiny goes forth from within people, not from without into them.

RAINER MARIA RILKE, from Letters to a Young Poet,
translation by M. D. Herter Norton

Understand, I'll slip quietly
away from the noisy crowd
when I see the pale
stars rising, blooming, over the oaks.

I'll pursue solitary pathways
through the pale twilit meadows,
with only this one dream:
You come too.

RAINER MARIA RILKE, from *First Poems*,
translation by M. D. Herter Norton

Oh,
I am thinking
Oh,
I am thinking
I have found
my lover.
Oh,
I think it is so.

Chippewa song

Night is a dead monotonous period under a roof; but in the open world it passes lightly, with its stars and dews and perfumes, and the hours are marked by changes in the face of Nature. What seems a kind of temporal death to people choked between walls and curtains, is only a light and living slumber to the man who sleeps afield. All night long he can hear Nature breathing deeply and freely; even as she takes her rest she turns and smiles; and there is one stirring hour unknown to those who dwell in houses, when a wakeful influence goes abroad over the sleeping hemisphere, and all the outdoor world are on their feet. It is then that the cock first crows, not this time to announce the dawn, but like a cheerful watchman speeding the course of night. Cattle awake on the hillside; sheep break their fast on dewy hillsides, and change to a new lair among the ferns; and houseless men, who have lain down with the fowls, open their dim eyes and behold the beauty of the night.

At what inaudible summons, at what gentle touch of Nature, are all these sleepers thus recalled in the same hour to life? Do the stars rain down an influence, or do we share some thrill of mother earth below our resting bodies? Even shepherds and old country-folk, who are the deepest read in these arcana, have not a guess as to the means or purpose of this nightly resurrection. Towards two in the morning they declare the thing takes place; and neither know nor inquire further. . . .

When that hour came to me among the pines, I wakened thirsty. My tin was standing by me half full of water. I emptied it at a draught; and feeling broad awake after this internal cold aspersion, sat upright to make a cigarette. The stars were clear, coloured, and jewel-like, but not frosty. A faint silvery vapour stood for the Milky Way. All around me the black fir-points stood upright and stock-still. . . . I lay lazily smoking and studying the colour of the sky, as we call the void of space, from where it showed a reddish gray behind the pines to where it showed a glossy blue-black between the stars. . . . And yet even while I was exulting in my solitude I became aware of a strange lack. I wished a companion to lie near me in the starlight, silent and not moving, but ever within touch. For there is a fellowship more quiet even than solitude, and which, rightly understood, is solitude made perfect. And to live out of doors with the woman a man loves is of all lives the most complete and free.

ROBERT LOUIS STEVENSON, from "A Night Among the Pines"

Go seek her out all courteously,
And say I come,
Wind of spices whose song is ever
Epithalamium.
O hurry over the dark lands
And run upon the sea
For seas and land shall not divide us
My love and me.

Now, wind, of your good courtesy
I pray you go,
And come into her little garden
And sing at her window;
Singing: The bridal wind is blowing
For Love is at his noon;
And soon will your true love be with you,
Soon, O soon.

JAMES JOYCE, poem XIII from *Chamber Music*

[*Mr. Emerson, to Lucy:*] "I used to think I could teach young people the whole of life, but I know better now, and all my teaching has come down to this: beware of muddle. . . . Though life is very glorious, it is difficult. . . . Man has to pick up the use of his functions as he goes along—especially the function of love. . . .

"You must marry, or your life will be wasted. You have gone too far to retreat. I have no time for the tenderness, and the comradeship, and the poetry, and the things that really matter, and *for which* you marry. I know that, with George, you will find them and that you love him. Then be his wife. He is already part of you. Though you fly to Greece, and never see him again, or forget his very name, George will work in your thoughts till you die. It isn't possible to love and to part. You will wish that it was. You can transmute love, ignore it, muddle it, but you can never pull it out of you . . . love is eternal. . . .

"I only wish poets would say this, too: love is of the body; not the body but of the body. Ah! the misery that would be saved if we confessed that! . . . When I think what life is, and how seldom love is answered by love— Marry him; it is one of the moments for which the world was made. . . .

"Now it is all dark. Now Beauty and Passion seem never to have existed. I know. But remember the mountains over Florence, and the view. . . . Yes, we fight for more than Love or Pleasure; there is Truth. Truth counts. Truth does count."

E. M. FORSTER, from *A Room with a View*

The crossing of the threshold is the first step into the sacred zone of the universal source.

JOSEPH CAMPBELL, from *The Hero with a Thousand Faces*

Oh, hasten not this loving act,
Rapture where self and not-self meet:
My life has been the awaiting you,
Your footfall was my own heart's beat.

PAUL VALÉRY

Apparently I am going to marry Charles Lindbergh. It must seem hysterically funny to you as it did to me, when I consider my opinions on marriage. "A safe marriage," "things in common," "liking the same things," "a quiet life," etc., etc. All those things which I am apparently going against. But they seem to have lost their meaning, or have other definitions. Isn't it funny—*why does* one marry, anyway? I didn't expect or want anything like this. . . .

Don't wish me happiness—I don't expect to be happy, but it's gotten beyond that, somehow. Wish me courage and strength and a sense of humor—I will need them all. . . .

ANNE MORROW LINDBERGH, from *Bring Me a Unicorn*

. . . Really I began the day
Not with a man's wish: "May this day be different";
But with the bird's wish: "May this day
Be the same day, the day of my life."

RANDALL JARRELL, from "A Man Meets a Woman in the Street"

The very earth will disown you
If your soul barter my soul;
In angry tribulation
The waters will tremble and rise.
My world become more beautiful
Since the day you took me to you,

When, under the flowering thorn tree
Together we stood without words,
And love, like the heavy fragrance
Of the flowering thorn tree, pierced us. . . .
The kiss your mouth gives another
Will echo within my ear,

As the deep surrounding caverns
Bring back your words to me.

Even the dust of the highway
Keeps the scent of your footprints.
I track them, and like a deer
Follow you into the mountains.

Clouds will paint over my dwelling
The image of your new love.
Go to her like a thief, crawling
In the boweled earth to kiss her.
When you lift her face you will find
My face disfigured with weeping.

God will not give you the light
Unless you walk by my side.
God will not let you drink
If I do not tremble in the water.
He will not let you sleep
Except in the hollow of my hair.

If you go, you destroy my soul
As you trample the weeds by the roadside.
Hunger and thirst will gnaw you,
Crossing the heights or the plains;
And wherever you are, you will watch
The evenings bleed with my wounds.

When you call another woman
I will issue forth on your tongue,
Even as a taste of salt
Deep in the roots of your throat.
In hating, or singing, in yearning
It is me alone you summon. . . .

GABRIELA MISTRAL, "God Wills It,"
translation by K.G.C.

Will you perhaps consent to be
Now that a little while is still
(Ruth of sweet wind) now that a little while
My mind's continuing and unreleasing wind
Touches this single of your flowers, this one only,
Will you perhaps consent to be
My many-branched, small and dearest tree?

My mind's continuing and unreleasing wind
—The wind which is wild and restless, tired and asleep,
The wind which is tired, wild and still continuing,
The wind which is chill, and warm, wet, soft, in every
        influence,
Lusts for Paris, Crete and Pergamus,
Is suddenly off for Paris and Chicago,
Judaea, San Francisco, the Midi
—May I perhaps return to you
Wet with an Attic dust and chill from Norway
My dear, so-many-branched smallest tree?

Would you perhaps consent to be
The very rack and crucifix of winter, winter's wild
Knife-edged, continuing and unreleasing,
Intent and stripping, ice-caressing wind?
My dear, most dear, so-many-branched tree,
My mind's continuing and unreleasing wind
Touches this single of your flowers, faith in me,
Wide as the—sky!—accepting as the (air)!
—Consent, consent, consent to be
My many-branched, small and dearest tree.

DELMORE SCHWARTZ, "Will you perhaps consent to be"
("méntre il vento, come fa, si tace")

Nothing is plumb, level or square:
　　the studs are bowed, the joists
are shaky by nature, no piece fits
　　any other piece without a gap
or pinch, and bent nails
　　dance all over the surfacing
like maggots. By Christ
　　I am no carpenter. I built
the roof for myself, the walls
　　for myself, the floors
for myself, and got
　　hung up in it myself. I
danced with a purple thumb
　　at this house-warming, drunk
with my prime whiskey: rage.
　　Oh I spat rage's nails
into the frame-up of my work:
　　it held. It settled plumb,
level, solid, square and true
　　for that great moment. Then
it screamed and went on through,
　　skewing as wrong the other way.
God damned it. This is hell,
　　but I planned it, I sawed it,
I nailed it, and I
　　will live in it until it kills me.
I can nail my left palm
　　to the left-hand cross-piece but
I can't do everything myself.
　　I need a hand to nail the right,
a help, a love, a you, a wife.

ALAN DUGAN, "Love Song: I and Thou"

There came you wishing me * * *
And so I said * * *
And then you turned your head
With the greatest beauty

Smiting me mercilessly!
And then you said * * *
So that my heart was made
Into the strangest country . . .

* * * you said, so beauteously,
So that an angel came
To hear that name,
And we caught him tremulously!

José Garcia Villa, from
Have Come, Am Here,
translation by Ben F. Carruthers

As I was walking
      I came upon
chance walking
      the same road upon.

As I sat down
      by chance to move
later
      if and as I might,

light the wood was,
      light and green
and what I saw
      before I had not seen.

It was a lady
        accompanied
by goat men
        leading her.

Her hair held earth.
        Her eyes were dark.
A double flute
        made her move.

"O love,
        where are you
leading
        me now?"

ROBERT CREELEY, "Kore"

". . . dear beast, you shall not die," said Beauty. "You will live
in order to become my husband. From this moment on, I give
you my hand and I swear that I shall be yours alone. Alas! I
thought that I felt only friendship for you, but the sorrow that
I feel now makes me see that I cannot live without you."

Hardly had Beauty spoken these words when she saw the
castle blazing with lights—there were fireworks and music and
everything to indicate a celebration. None of these wonders
held her attention, however; she turned her eyes back toward
her dear beast. . . . But to her surprise, the beast had disappeared
and at her feet she saw instead a prince handsomer than the
god of love, who thanked her for having ended his enchantment.
Although this prince deserved all her attention, she could not
help asking where the beast was.

"You see him at your feet," the prince told her. "A wicked

fairy had condemned me to remain in that shape until a beautiful girl should agree to marry me, and she had forbidden me to reveal my wit and intelligence. You were the only person in the world good enough to let yourself be moved by the goodness of my character, and in offering you my crown, I am only freeing myself of my obligations to you."

Beauty, pleasantly surprised, gave her hand to this handsome prince to help him to rise. They went together to the castle, and Beauty almost died of joy to find in the great hall her father and all her family, transported to the castle by the beautiful lady who had appeared to her in a dream.

"Beauty," said the lady, who was a powerful fairy, "come and receive the reward of your good choice. You have preferred virtue to handsomeness and wit and you deserve to find all these qualities united in one single person. You are going to become a great queen. . . ."

Saying this, the fairy waved her wand, and everyone who was in the hall was transported to the prince's kingdom. His subjects received him with joy, and he married Beauty, who lived with him for a long time in a state of happiness that was perfect because it was based upon virtue.

MADAME LePRINCE DE BEAUMONT, from "Beauty and the Beast,"
translation by Alfred and Mary Elizabeth David

I have always known
That at last I would
Take this road, but yesterday
I did not know that it would be today.

KENNETH REXROTH, from *One Hundred Poems
from the Japanese*

II

In Search of Love

Did you ever seek God?
No.

What is it that you sought?
I sought love.

And you sought love for what reason?
Those about me, from childhood on, had sought love. I heard
and saw them. I saw them rise and fall on that wave. I closely
overheard and sharply overlooked their joy and grief. I worked
from memory and example.

LOUISE BOGAN, from *Journey Around My Room*

ove is the flame that leads a person from solitude to a state of union, and the wedding is the "ritual of passage" between. For thousands of years, poets and philosophers have tried to define this condition of mind and body and to measure its power to impel a person out of one life into another. A selection of their meditations follows, offering possible additions to traditional Western wedding liturgies.

Some of these passages, like those from the King James translation of 1 Corinthians, are phrased in the lovely old cadences of traditional scripture. Others, like the New English Bible version of Corinthians, address the ancient question in language of plain speech as it is used today by what the poet Wallace Stevens calls "the men of the time . . . and the women of the time." These men and women are ourselves, no less drawn than our ancestors were to the ideals of generosity, permanence, and mutual trust which marriage implies.

Aristophanes: . . . Love is the oldest of the gods, and he is also the source of the greatest benefits to us. . . .

Original human nature was not like the present but different. The sexes were not two as they are now but originally three in number; there was man, woman, and the union of the two. . . . the man was originally the child of the sun, the woman of the earth, and the man-woman of the moon, which is made up of sun and earth. . . . [Now] when one of them meets his other half, the actual half of himself, the pair are lost in an amazement of love and friendship and intimacy. . . . these are the people who pass their whole lives together. . . . The reason is that human nature was originally one and we were a whole, and the desire and pursuit of the whole is called love. . . .

I believe that if our loves were perfectly accomplished, and each one returning to his primeval nature had his original true love, then our race would be happy. . . . [Therefore] we must praise the god Love, who is our greatest benefactor, both leading us in this life back to our own nature, and giving us high hopes for the future, for he promises that if we are pious, he will restore us to our original state, and heal us, and make us happy and blessed.

Agathon: . . . [Love is rather] the youngest of the gods and youthful ever. . . . had Love been in [the old] days, there would have been no . . . violence but peace and sweetness as there is now in heaven, since the rule of Love began. Love is young and also tender. . . . he walks not upon the earth nor yet upon the skulls of men . . . but in the hearts and souls of both gods and men, which are of all things the softest: in them he walks and dwells and makes his home. Not in every soul without exception, for where there is hardness he departs, where there is softness there he dwells . . . he dwells in the place of flowers and scents, there he sits and abides. . . .

His greatest glory is that he can neither do nor suffer wrong to or from any god or any man; . . . all men in all things serve him of their own free will, and where there is voluntary agreement, there, as the laws which are the lords of the city say, is justice. . . .

Of his courage and justice and temperance I have spoken, but I have yet to speak of his wisdom . . . : he is a poet and also the source of poesy in others. . . . at the touch of him every one becomes a poet even though he had no music in him before. . . .

As to the artists, do we not know that he only of them whom love inspires has the light of fame? He whom Love touches not walks in darkness. . . .

[He is] the friend of the good, the wonder of the wise, the amazement of the gods . . . parent of delicacy, luxury, desire, fondness, softness, grace; regardful of the good, regardless of the evil . . . saviour, pilot, comrade, helper . . . leader best and brightest in whose footsteps let every man follow, sweetly singing in his honor and joining in that sweet strain with which love charms the souls of gods and men.

Socrates: . . . [Love] is a great spirit intermediate between the divine and the mortal. . . . He is neither mortal nor immortal but alive and flourishing at one moment when he is in plenty and dead at another moment and again alive. . . . that which is always flowing in is always flowing out, and so he is never in want and never in wealth. . . . Wisdom is a most beautiful thing,

and Love is of the beautiful; and therefore Love is also a philosopher or lover of wisdom. . . . love is the love of the everlasting possession of the good. . . . love is of immortality. . . .
love begins with the desire of union. . . .

And the true order of going, or being led by another, to the
things of love, is to begin from the beauties of earth and mount
upwards for the sake of . . . absolute beauty . . . that life above
all others which a man should live, in the contemplation of
beauty absolute.

. . . of this end human nature will not easily find a helper
better than love. And therefore I say that every man ought to
honor him, and walk in his ways and exhort others to do the
same, and praise the power and spirit of love . . . now and ever.

PLATO, from the Symposium, translation by Benjamin Jowett

Though I speak with the tongues of men and of angels, and
have not charity, I am become as sounding brass, or a tinkling
cymbal.

2   And though I have the gift of prophecy, and understand
all mysteries, and all knowledge; and though I have all faith,
so that I could remove mountains, and have not charity, I am
nothing.

3   And though I bestow all my goods to feed the poor, and
though I give my body to be burned, and have not charity, it
profiteth me nothing.

4   Charity suffereth long, and is kind; charity envieth not;
charity vaunteth not itself, is not puffed up,

5   Doth not behave itself unseemly, seeketh not her own,
is not easily provoked, thinketh no evil;

6   Rejoiceth not in iniquity, but rejoiceth in the truth;

7 Beareth all things, believeth all things, hopeth all things, endureth all things.

8 Charity never faileth: but whether there be prophecies, they shall fail; whether there be tongues, they shall cease; whether there be knowledge, it shall vanish away.

9 For we know in part, and we prophesy in part.

10 But when that which is perfect is come, then that which is in part shall be done away.

11 When I was a child, I spake as a child, I understood as a child, I thought as a child: but when I became a man, I put away childish things.

12 For now we see through a glass, darkly; but then face to face: now I know in part; but then shall I know even as also I am known.

13 And now abideth faith, hope, charity, these three; but the greatest of these is charity.

1 Corinthians 13 (King James Version)

Love is patient and kind; love is not jealous or boastful; it is not arrogant or rude. Love does not insist on its own way; it is not irritable or resentful; it does not rejoice at wrong, but rejoices in the right. Love bears all things, believes all things, hopes all things, endures all things. Love never ends.

1 Corinthians 13:4–8a (New English Bible)

All happiness or unhappiness solely depends upon the quality of the object to which we are attached by love. Love for an object eternal and infinite feeds the mind with joy alone, a joy that is free from all sorrow.

Baruch Spinoza

Emily Dickinson

611

I see thee better - in the Dark -
I do not need a Light -
The Love of Thee - a Prism be -
Excelling Violet - . . .

What need of Day -
To Those whose Dark - hath so - surpassing Sun -
It deem it be - Continually -
At the Meridian?

917

Love - is anterior to Life -
Posterior - to Death -
Initial of Creation, and
The Exponent of Earth.

1155

Distance - is not the Realm of Fox
Nor by Relay of Bird
Abated - Distance is
Until thyself, Beloved.

from *The Complete Poems*,
edited by Thomas H. Johnson

William Shakespeare

XVIII

Shall I compare thee to a summer's day?
Thou art more lovely and more temperate:
Rough winds do shake the darling buds of May,
And summer's lease hath all too short a date:
Sometimes too hot the eye of heaven shines,
And often is his gold complexion dimm'd,
And every fair from fair sometime declines,
By chance, or nature's changing course, untrim'd,
But thy eternal summer shall not fade,
Nor loose possession of that fair thou ow'st,
Nor shall death brag thou wandr'st in his shade,
When in eternal lines to time thou grow'st,
    So long as men can breathe, or eyes can see,
    So long lives this, and this gives life to thee.

XXX

When to the sessions of sweet silent thought
I summon up remembrance of things past,
I sigh the lack of many a thing I sought,
And with old woes new wail my dear times' waste:
Then can I drown an eye, unus'd to flow,
For precious friends hid in death's dateless night,
And weep afresh love's long since cancell'd woe,
And moan the expense of many a vanish'd sight:
Then can I grieve at grievances foregone,
And heavily from woe to woe tell o'er
The sad account of fore-bemoaned moan,
Which I new pay as if not paid before.
    But if the while I think on thee, dear friend,
    All losses are restor'd and sorrows end.

XXXI

Thy bosom is endeared with all hearts,
Which I by lacking have supposed dead;
And there reigns love and all love's loving parts,
And all those friends which I thought buried.
How many a holy and obsequious tear
Hath dear religious love stolen from mine eye,
As interest of the dead, which now appear,
But things remov'd that hidden in there lie.
Thou art the grave where buried love doth live
Hung with the trophies of my lovers gone
Who all their parts of me to thee did give;
That due of many now is thine alone.
    Their images I loved I view in thee
    And thou, all they, hast all the all of me.

CXVI

Let me not to the marriage of true minds
Admit impediments. Love is not love
Which alters when it alteration finds,
Or bends with the remover to remove:
O, no! it is an ever-fixed mark,
That looks on tempests and is never shaken;
It is the star to every wandering bark,
Whose worth's unknown, although his height be taken.
Love's not Time's fool, though rosy lips and cheeks
Within his bending sickle's compass come;
Love alters not with his brief hours and weeks,
But bears it out even to the edge of doom.
    If this is error, and upon me prov'd,
    I never writ, nor no man ever lov'd.

When in the chronicle of wasted time
I see descriptions of the fairest wights,
And beauty making beautiful old rhyme
In praise of ladies dead and lovely knights,
Then, in the blazon of sweet beauty's best,
Of hand, of foot, of lip, of eye, of brow,
I see their antique pen would have express'd
Even such a beauty as you master now.
So all their praises are but prophecies
Of this our time, all you prefiguring;
And, for they look'd but with divining eyes,
They had not skill enough your worth to sing:
      For we, which now behold these present days,
      Have eyes to wonder, but lack tongues to praise.

SHAKESPEARE, *Sonnets*

The passion which unites the sexes . . . is habitually spoken of as though it were a simple feeling; whereas it is the most compound, and therefore the most powerful, of all the feelings. Added to the purely physical elements of it are first to be noticed those highly complex impressions produced by personal beauty, around which are aggregated a variety of pleasurable ideas, not in themselves amatory, but which have an organised relation to the amatory feeling. With this there is united the complex sentiment which we term affection—a sentiment which, as it can exist between those of the same sex, must be regarded as an independent sentiment, but one which is here greatly exalted.

Then there is the sentiment of admiration, respect, or reverence; in itself one of considerable power, and which, in this relation, becomes in a high degree active. Then comes next the feeling called love of approbation. To be preferred above all the world, and that by one admired beyond all others, is to have the love of approbation gratified in a degree passing every previous experience. . . . Further, the allied emotion of self-esteem comes into play. To have succeeded in gaining such attachment from, and sway over, another, is a proof of power which cannot fail agreeably to excite the *amour propre*. Yet again, the proprietary feeling has its share in the general activity: there is the pleasure of possession; the two belong to each other. Once more, the relation allows of an extended liberty of action. Towards other persons a restrained behaviour is requisite. Round each there is a subtle boundary that may not be crossed—an individuality on which none may trespass. But in this case the barriers are thrown down, and thus the love of unrestrained activity is gratified. Finally, there is an exaltation of the sympathies. Egoistic pleasures of all kinds are doubled by another's sympathetic participation, and the pleasures of another are added to the egoistic pleasures. Thus, round the physical feeling forming the nucleus of the whole, are gathered the feelings produced by personal beauty; that constituting simple attachment, those of reverence, of love of approbation, of self-esteem, of property, of love of freedom, of sympathy. These, all greatly exalted, and severally tending to reflect their excitements on one another, unite to form the mental state we call love. And as each of them is of itself comprehensive of multitudinous states of consciousness, we may say that this passion fuses into one immense aggregate most of the elementary excitations of which we are capable; and that hence results in irresistible power.

HERBERT SPENCER, from *The Principles of Psychology*

It may be asked, is love necessary to man? This is not a matter for reasoning, but for feeling. We deliberate not upon it; we are carried irresistibly towards the conclusion; and we deceive ourselves when we make it a subject for discussion.

Purity (*netteté*) of spirit produces corresponding purity of passion; therefore it is, that a pure and elevated mind loves with intenseness, and has an intense perception of the qualities which excite its ardours.

Who then can doubt that we exist only to love? Disguise it, in fact, as we will, we love without intermission. Where we seem most effectually to shut out love, it lies covert and concealed: we live not a moment exempt from its influence.

Man cannot find his satisfactions within himself only; and, as love is essential to him, he must seek the objects of his affection in external objects. He can find these only in beauty; but as he himself is the fairest being that the hand of God has formed, he must look within himself for a model of those beauties which he seeks elsewhere. . . . Such is the largeness of his heart, that it must be something resembling himself, and approximating to his own qualities. That kind of beauty, therefore, which satisfies man, must not only contribute to his enjoyment, but partake of his own resemblance. It is restricted and fulfilled in the difference of the sexes.

Nature has so impressed this truth upon our minds, that we all find a predisposition towards it; it demands no skill or research for its discovery; we find a void within the bosom, and this it is which fills it. . . .

When a person is in love, he seems to himself wholly changed from what he was before; and he fancies that everybody sees him in the same light. This is a great mistake; but reason being obscured by passion, he cannot be convinced, and goes on still under the delusion. . . .

It has been usual, but without cause, to underrate, and regard, as opposed to reason, the passion of love. Reason and love are, however, consistent with each other. It is a precipitation of mind that thus carries us into partialities and extremes; but it is still reason, and we ought not to wish it to be otherwise. We should, in that case, only prove man to be a very disagreeable machine. Let us not seek to exclude reason from love; for they are inseparable. . . .

It is with love as with the understanding; one person supposes he has as much sense as another, and can love as well as another. But a mind of refinement carries its attachments into the minutest things, and this is not the case with others. It requires, however, a delicate perception to mark this difference.

Under the influence of strong passion the beloved object seems new in every interview. Absence instantaneously creates a void in the heart. But then, the joys of reunion!

BLAISE PASCAL, from "On the Passion of the Soul,"
translation by George Pearce

The memories of long love
Gather like drifting snow,
Poignant as the mandarin ducks,
who float side by side in sleep.

.   .   .

Falling from the ridge
Of high Tsukuba,
The Minano River
At last gathers itself,
Like my love, into
A deep, still pool.

KENNETH REXROTH, from *One Hundred
Poems from the Japanese*

John Keats

[July 1, 1819]

. . . Ask yourself my love whether you are not very cruel to have so entrammelled me, so destroyed my freedom. Will you confess this in the Letter you must write immediately and do all you can to console me in it—make it rich as a draught of poppies to intoxicate me—write the softest words and kiss them that I may at least touch my lips where yours have been. For myself I know not how to express my devotion to so fair a form: I want a brighter word than bright, a fairer word than fair. I almost wish we were butterflies and liv'd but three summer days—three such days with you I could fill with more delight than fifty common years could ever contain. . . .

[July 8, 1819]

. . . Even when I am not thinking of you I receive your influence and a tenderer nature steeling upon me. All my thoughts, my unhappiest days and nights have I find not at all cured me of my love of Beauty, but made it so intense that I am miserable that you are not with me: or rather breathe in that dull sort of patience that cannot be called Life. I never knew before, what such a love as you have made me feel, was; I did not believe in it; my Fancy was affraid of it, lest it should burn me up. But if you will fully love me, though there may be some fire, 't will not be more than we can bear when moistened and bedewed with Pleasures. . . . I would never see any thing but Pleasure in your eyes, love on your lips, and Happiness in your steps. I would wish to see you among those amusements suitable to your inclinations and spirits; so that our loves might be a delight in the midst of Pleasures agreeable enough, rather than a resource from vexations and cares—But I doubt much, in case of the worst, whether I shall be philosopher enough to follow my own Lessons: if I saw my resolution give you a pain I could not. Why may I not speak of your Beauty, since without that I could never have lov'd you—I cannot conceive any beginning of such love as I have for you but Beauty. There may be a sort of love for which, without the least sneer at it, I have the highest respect, and can admire it in others: but it has not the richness, the bloom, the full form, the enchantment of love after my own heart. So let me speak of you Beauty, though to my own endangering; if you could be so cruel to me as to try elsewhere its Power. You say you are affraid I shall think you do not love me—in saying this you make me ache the more to be near you. . . .

[March 1820]

Sweetest Fanny,

You fear, sometimes, I do not love you so much as you wish? My dear Girl I love you ever and ever and without reserve. The more I have known you the more have I lov'd. In every way—even my jealousies have been agonies of Love, in the hottest fit I ever had I would have died for you. I have vex'd you too much. But for Love! Can I help it? You are always new. The last of your kisses was ever the sweetest; the last smile the brightest; the last movement the gracefullest. When you pass'd my window home yesterday, I was fill'd with as much admiration as if I had then seen you for the first time. You uttered a half complaint once that I only lov'd your Beauty. Have I nothing else then to love in you but that? Do not I see a heart naturally furnish'd with wings imprison itself with me? No ill prospect has been able to turn your thoughts a moment from me. This perhaps should be as much a subject of sorrow as joy—but I will not talk of that. Even if you did not love me I could not help an entire devotion to you: how much more deeply then must I feel for you knowing you love me. My Mind has been the most discontented and restless one that ever was put into a body too small for it. I never felt my Mind repose upon anything with complete and undistracted enjoyment—upon no person but you. When you are in the room my thoughts never fly out of window: you always concentrate my whole senses. The anxiety shown about our Loves in your last note is an immense pleasure to me: however you must not suffer such speculations to molest you any more: nor will I any more believe you can have the least pique against me. . . .

[June 1820]

. . . My head is puzzled this morning, and I scarce know what I shall say though I am full of a hundred things. 'T is certain I would rather be writing to you this morning, notwithstanding the alloy of grief in such an occupation, than enjoy any other pleasure, with health to boot, unconnected with you. Upon my soul I have loved you to the extreme. I wish you could know the Tenderness with which I continually brood over your different aspects of countenance, action and dress. I see you come down in the morning: I see you meet me at the Window—I see every thing over again eternally that I ever have seen. If I get on the pleasant clue I live in a sort of happy misery, if on the unpleasant 'tis miserable misery. You complain of my ill-treating you in word thought and deed—I am sorry,—at times I feel bitterly sorry that I ever made you unhappy—my excuse is that those words have been wrung from me by the sha[r]pness of my feelings. At all events and in any case I have been wrong; could I believe that I did it without any cause, I should be the most sincere of Penitents. I could give way to my repentant feelings now, I could recant all my suspicions, I could mingle with you heart and Soul though absent, were it not for some parts of your Letters. Do you suppose it possible I could ever leave you? You know what I think of myself and what of you.

You know that I should feel how much it was my loss and how little yours. . . . do nothing but love me—if I knew that for certain life and health will in such event be a heaven, and death itself will be less painful. I long to believe in immortality I shall never be ab[le] to bid you an entire farewell. If I am destined to be happy with you here—how short is the longest Life— I wish to believe in immortality—I wish to live with you for ever. . . .

Excerpts of letters to Fanny Brawne

Ah Love! could you and I with Him conspire
To grasp this sorry Scheme of Things entire,
Would not we shatter it to bits—and then
Remold it nearer to the Heart's desire!

EDWARD FITZGERALD, from
The Rubáiyát of Omar Khayyám

. . . Ah, love, let us be true
To one another! for the world, which seems
To lie before us like a land of dreams,
So various, so beautiful, so new,
Hath really neither joy, nor love, nor light,
Nor certitude, nor peace, nor help for pain;
And we are here as on a darkling plain
Swept with confused alarms of struggle and flight
Where ignorant armies clash by night.

MATTHEW ARNOLD, from "Dover Beach"

Ralph Waldo Emerson

Give all to love;
Obey thy heart;
Friends, kindred, days,
Estate, good-fame,
Plans, credit and the Muse,
Nothing refuse.

'Tis a brave master;
Let it have scope:
Follow it utterly,
Hope beyond hope:
High and more high
It dives into noon,
With wing unspent,
Untold intent;
But it is a god,
Knows its own path
And the outlets of the sky.

It was never for the mean;
It requireth courage stout.
Souls above doubt,
Valour unbending.
It will reward,
They shall return
More than they were,
And ever ascending. . . .

from "Give All to Love"

. . . All mankind loves a lover. . . . [Love] is the dawn of civility and grace. . . . Persons are love's world, and the coldest philosopher cannot recount the debt of the young soul wandering here in nature to the power of love . . . though the celestial rapture falling out of heaven seizes only upon those of tender age . . . yet the remembrance of these visions outlasts all other remembrances, and is a wreath of flowers on the oldest brows. . . .

No man ever forgot the visitations of that power to his heart and brain, which created all things new; which was the dawn in him of music, poetry and art; which made the face of nature radiant with purple light; the morning and the night varied enchantments; when a single tone of one voice could make the heart beat, and the most trivial circumstance associated with one form is put in the amber of memory; when we became all eye when one was present; and all memory when one was gone; . . . for the figures, the motions, the words of the beloved object are not like other images written in water, but, as Plutarch said, "enameled in fire." . . .

The passion remakes the world. . . . It makes all things alive and significant. . . . Every bird on the boughs of the trees sings now to his heart and soul. Almost, the notes are articulate. The clouds have faces . . . the trees, the waving grass and the flowers have grown intelligent. . . . Behold the fine madman! He is a palace of sweet sounds and sights . . . he is twice a man . . . he feels the blood of the violet, the clover and the lily in his veins; and he talks with the brook that wets his foot. . . .

The like force has the passion over all his nature. It expands the sentiment; it makes the clown gentle and gives the coward heart. Into the most pitiful and abject it will infuse a heart and courage to defy the world. . . . In giving him to another it still more gives him to himself. He is a new man with new perceptions, new and keener purposes. . . .

Love prays. It makes covenants with Eternal Power . . . the union which is thus affected . . . adds a new value to every atom in nature, for it transmutes every thread throughout the whole web of relation into a golden ray and bathes the soul in a new and sweeter element . . . it is the nature and end of this relation, that [the lovers] should represent the human race to each other. All that is in the world . . . is cunningly wrought into the texture of man, of woman. . . .

The world rolls; the circumstances vary every hour. . . . [The lovers'] once flaming regard is sobered . . . and losing in violence what it gains in extent, it becomes a thorough good understanding. At last [the lovers] discover that all which at first drew them together—those once sacred features, that magical play of charms—had a prospective end, like the scaffolding by which the house was built, and the purification of the intellect and the heart, from year to year, is the real marriage. . . .

Thus we are put in training for a love which knows not sex, nor person, nor partiality but which seeketh virtue and wisdom everywhere, to the end of increasing virtue and wisdom. . . . We are often made to feel that our affections are but tents of a night. . . . But in health, the mind is presently seen again— its overarching vault, bright with galaxies of immutable lights, and the warm loves and fears that swept over us as clouds. . . . But we need not fear that we can lose anything by the progress of the soul. The soul may be trusted to the end. That which is so beautiful and attractive as these relations must be succeeded and supplanted only by what is more beautiful, and so on forever.

from his essay "Love"

. . . he's more myself than I am. Whatever our souls are made of, his and mine are the same. . . . If all else perished and *he* remained, I should still continue to be, and if all else remained, and he were annihilated, the universe would turn to a might stranger. . . . He's always, always in my mind; not as a pleasure to myself, but as my own being.

EMILY BRONTË, from Wuthering Heights

. . . our love it was stronger by far than the love
    Of those who were older than we—
    Of many far wiser than we—
And neither the angels in Heaven above,
    Nor the demons down under the sea,
Can ever dissever my soul from the soul
    Of the beautiful Annabel Lee:—

For the moon never beams without bringing me dreams
    Of the beautiful Annabel Lee;
And the stars never rise but I feel the bright eyes
    Of the beautiful Annabel Lee.
And so, all the night-tide, I lie down by the side
Of my darling, my darling, my life and my bride. . . .

EDGAR ALLAN POE, from "Annabel Lee"

. . . our love is a portion of our soul more lasting than the various selves which die successively in us and which would selfishly like to retain this love—a portion of our soul which, regardless of the useful suffering this may cause us, must detach itself from its human objects in order to make clear to us and restore its quality of generality and give this love, an understanding of this love, to all the world, to the universal intelligence, and not first to this woman, then to that, in whom this one and that of our successive selves seek to lose their identity.

MARCEL PROUST, from *The Past Recaptured*,
translation by Frederick A. Blossom

To love is good; love being difficult. For one human being to love another; that is perhaps the most difficult of all our tasks, the ultimate, the last test and proof, the work for which all other work is but preparation. For this reason [beginners] cannot yet know love: they have to learn it. . . . Learning-time is always a long, secluded time, and so loving, for a long while ahead and far on into life, is—solitude, intensified and deepened loneness for him who loves. . . . it is a high inducement to the individual to ripen, to become something in himself, to become world, to become world for himself for another's sake, it is a great exacting claim upon him, something that chooses him out and calls him to vast things. Only in this sense, as the task of working at themselves ("to hearken and to hammer day and night") might young people use the love that is given them.

RAINER MARIA RILKE, from *Letters to a Young Poet*,
translation by M. D. Herter Norton

What thou lovest well remains,
   the rest is dross
What thou lov'st well shall not be
   reft from thee
What thou lov'st well is thy true
   heritage. . . .

EZRA POUND, from *The Cantos*

Be in me as the eternal moods
        of the bleak wind, and not
As transient things are—
        gaiety of flowers.
Have me in the strong loneliness
        of sunless cliffs
And of grey waters.
        Let the gods speak softly of us
In days hereafter,
        The shadowy flowers of Orcus
Remember Thee.

EZRA POUND, "ΔΩΡIA"

Love is a battle. Love is war. Love is growing up.

JAMES BALDWIN, quoted in a statement by
his family to the press after his death

Romantic love is eternally alive; as the self's most urgent quest, as grail of our hopes of happiness, as the untarnished source of the tragic, the exalted, the extreme and the beautiful in modern life. The late twentieth century is the first to open itself up to the promise of love as the focus of universal aspirations. . . .

In the marriage ceremony, that moment when falling in love is replaced by the arduous drama of staying in love, the words "in sickness and in health, for richer, for poorer, till death do us part" set love in the temporal context in which it achieves its meaning. As time begins to elapse, one begins to love the other because they have shared the same experience. . . . Selves may not intertwine; but lives do, and shared memory becomes as much of a bond as the bond of the flesh. . . .

Family love is this dynastic awareness of time, this shared belonging to a chain of generations. . . . we collaborate together to root each other in a dimension of time longer than our own lives.

Michael Ignatieff, from "Lodged in the Heart and Memory"

Locate *I*
love you some-
where in

teeth and
eyes, bite
it but

take care not
to hurt, you
want so

much so
little. Words
say everything,

I
love you
again,

then what
is emptiness
for. To

fill, fill.
I heard words
and words full

of holes
aching. Speech
is a mouth.

ROBERT CREELEY,
"The Language"

. . . It has to be living, to learn the speech of the place.
It has to face the men of the time and to meet
The women of the time. It has to think about war
And it has to find what will suffice. It has
To construct a new stage. It has to be on that stage
And, like an insatiable actor, slowly and
With meditation, speak words that in the ear,
In the delicatest ear of the mind, repeat,
Exactly, that which it wants to hear, at the sound
Of which, an invisible audience listens,
Not to the play, but to itself, expressed
In an emotion as of two people, as of two
Emotions becoming one . . .

WALLACE STEVENS, from "Of Modern Poetry"

III

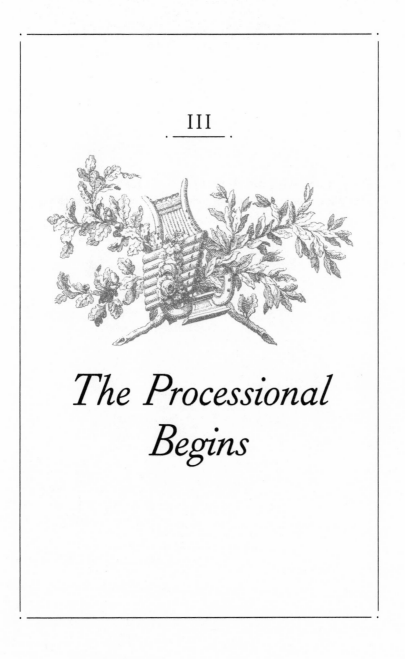

The Processional Begins

Here in the body pent, absent from Him I roam,
Yet nightly pitch my moving tent, a day's march nearer Home.

from a Moravian hymn

The wedding ceremony is a "ritual of passage" between two distinct worlds: the world of solitude and that of union. To traverse the distance between, as on any voyage, is to experience some anxiety and to pay a price. In the romantic-sounding language of depth psychology, the traveler will be called on to relinquish his or her old self so a new one may be reborn—that is, to exchange certain satisfactions for new and deeper ones. The readings which follow concern the passage across a psychic distance from an old life toward one to come. The Moravian hymn on the facing page expresses the pent-up energy and momentum of the journey, whether it be construed as toward one's heavenly "Home" or toward a new home for life.

Traversing the actual distance from the bride's house to a shrine or to her new home is still an event of extreme gravity today in much of Asia and Islam, where a girl may have been kept in seclusion for days or weeks before the event, then carried in a hooded palanquin to arrive, swathed in veils, before her husband. Even in the West, the start of the bridal processional is a moment of electric tension. In a synagogue, there may sound the shofar, or ram's horn, whose deep melancholy bleat was heard in ancient times in Canaan. A Christian church may fill with the jubilant chords of Mendelssohn's "Wedding March."

Ruth said:
"Intreat me not to leave thee,
    Or to return from following after thee:
For whither thou goest, I will go,
    And where thou lodgest, I will lodge.
Thy people shall be my people,
    And thy God my God.
Where thou diest, will I die,
    And there will I be buried.
The Lord do so to me, and more also,
    If ought but death part thee and me."

Ruth 1:16–17 (King James Version)

I will lead the blind men on their way
And guide them by paths they do not know.
I will turn darkness into light before them
And straighten their twisting roads.

Isaiah 42:16 (New English Bible)

Three nights of [pre]wedding festivities with their music and
gaiety expelled my melancholy and kept me from thinking of
what was to come. I laughed and was merry along with my
friends, so much so that the household interpreted my earlier

behaviour as nothing more than the ordinary display of fears common to prospective brides.

On the night of the wedding ceremony, the rapt attention focused upon me, especially by my friends, increased my joy so that I almost leaped with delight while I donned my wedding dress embroidered in thread of silver and gold. I was spellbound by the diamonds and other brilliant jewels that crowned my head and sparkled on my bodice and arms. All of this dazzled me and kept me from thinking of anything else. I was certain I would remain forever in this raiment, the centre of attention and admiration.

Presently, the singing girls appeared to escort me. My attendants supported me while the heavy jewels pressed down on my head and the wedding dress hung heavy on my small frame. I walked between rows of bright candles with rich scents wafting in the air, to the grand salon where I found a throng of women . . . in elegant gowns with jewels glittering on their heads, bosoms and arms. They all turned and looked at me with affection. When I raised my head to ease the heavy tiara back a little I heard a woman's voice whispering, "My daughter, lower your head and eyes." I then sat down on the bridal throne surrounded by flickering candles and decorated with flowers, fancying I was in another world. . . .

Next a dancer appeared and started to perform in front of me. She then made the rounds of the guests dancing in front of the women one at a time. They would take out coins, moisten them with their tongues and paste them on the dancer's forehead and cheeks. . . .

Suddenly, a commotion erupted outside the great hall. The dancer rushed out emitting a string of *zaghrudas*, the tremulous trills hanging in the air after her. To the roll of drums the women hastened out of the room or slipped behind curtains while the eunuch announced the approach of the bridegroom.

In an instant, the delicious dream vanished and stark reality appeared. Faint and crying, I clung to the gown of a relation—the wife of Ahmad Bey Hijazi—who was trying to flee like the others and I pleaded, "Don't abandon me here! Take me with you." My French tutor who was at my side embraced me and cried along with me murmuring, 'Have courage, my daughter, have courage.'" . . . Then a woman came and lowered a veil of silver thread over my head like a mask concealing the face of a condemned person approaching execution. At that moment, the bridegroom entered the room. After praying two *rakaas* on a mat of red velvet embossed with silver he came to me and, lifting the veil from my face, kissed me on the forehead. He led me by the hand to the bridal throne and took his place beside me. All the while, I was trembling like a branch in a storm. The groom addressed a few words to me but I understood nothing. . . . Finally, my new husband took me by the hand. In my daze I knew not where I was being led.

HUDA SHAARAWI, from *Harem Years: Memoirs of an Egyptian Feminist*,
translation by Margot Badran

The sun-beames in the East are spred,
Leave, leave, faire Bride, your solitary bed,
No more shall you returne to it alone,
It nourseth sadnesse, and your bodies print,
Like to a grave, the yielding downe doth dint;
You and your other you meet there anon;
Put forth, put forth that warme balm-breathing thigh,
Which when next time you in these sheets will smother,
There it must meet another . . .
Come glad from thence, goe gladder than you came,
Today put on perfection and a womans name . . .

The amorous evening starre is rose,
Why then should not our amorous starre inclose
Her selfe in her wish'd bed? . . . all toyl'd beasts
Rest duly; at night all their toyles are dispensed;
But in their beds commenced
Are other labours, and more dainty feasts;
She goes a maid, who, lest she turne the same
To night puts on perfection and a womans name.

Thy virgin's girdle now untie,
And in thy nuptiall bed (love's altar) lye
A pleasing sacrifice; now dispossesse
Thee of these chaines and robes which were put on
T'adorne the day, not thee; for thou, alone,
Like vertue'and truth, art best in nakednesse;
This bed is onely to virginitie
A grave, but, to a better state, a cradle;
Till now thou wast but able
To be what now thou art; then that by thee
No more be said, *I may bee*, but, *I am*,
To night put on perfection and a womans name. . . .

JOHN DONNE, from "Epithalamion Made at Lincoln's Inn"

Grow old along with me!
The best is yet to be,
The last of life, for which the first was made:
Our times are in his hand
Who saith, "A whole I planned,
Youth shows but half; trust God: see all, nor be afraid!" . . .

ROBERT BROWNING, from "Rabbi Ben Ezra"

I have a feeling that my boat
has struck, down there in the depths,
against a great thing.
                    And nothing
happens! Nothing . . . Silence . . . Waves . . .

—Nothing happens? Or has everything happened,
and are we standing now, quietly, in the new life?

Juan Ramón Jiménez, "Oceans,"
translation by Robert Bly

Here we are . . . on the roads of exodus. Far off in the distance,
the ground lets loose its aromatics. The country behind us winks
out in the blaze of daylight. The stripped earth bares its yellow
bones, graven with unknown ciphers. Where rye once bloomed,
and sorghum, white clay now smokes . . .

Our roads lie elsewhere . . . we move forward into God's
land like a starving tribe . . .

Before us rises the vision of our lives to come . . .

O weather of God, favor us . . .

The adventure is overwhelming, but we plunge toward it . . .

By the seven knit bones of the forehead and the face, let us
go forward, wearing ourselves to the bone, ah! even to the
splintering of the bone! . . .

God's dreams infuse us . . .

God's trickster, evil monkey, keep your distance!

Saint-Jean Perse, from "Drouth,"
translation by E. M.

Walt Whitman

Darest thou now O soul,
Walk out with me toward the unknown region,
Where neither ground is for the feet nor any path to follow?

No map there, nor guide,
Nor voice sounding, nor touch of human hand,
Nor face with blooming flesh, nor lips, nor eyes, are in that
     land.

I know it not O soul,
Nor dost thou, all is a blank before us,
All waits undream'd of in that region, that inaccessible
     land. . . .

from "Darest thou now O soul"

Are you the new person drawn toward me?
To begin with take warning, I am surely far different from what
     you suppose;
Do you suppose you will find in me your ideal?
Do you think it is so easy to have me become your lover?
Do you think the friendship of me would be unalloy'd
     satisfaction?
Do you think I am trusty and faithful?
Do you see no further than this façade, this smooth and tolerant
     manner of me?
Do you suppose yourself advancing on real ground toward a
     real heroic man?
Have you no thought O dreamer that it may be all maya,
     illusion?

"Are you the new person drawn toward me?"

Allons! whoever you are come travel with me!

Traveling with me you find what never tires.

The earth never tires,

The earth is rude, silent, incomprehensible at first, Nature is
    rude and incomprehensible at first,

Be not discouraged, keep on, there are divine things well
    envelop'd,

I swear to you there are divine things more beautiful than words
    can tell.

Allons! we must not stop here,

However sweet these laid-up stores, however convenient this
    dwelling we cannot remain here,

However shelter'd this port and however calm these waters we
    must not anchor here,

However welcome the hospitality that surrounds us we are
    permitted to receive it but a little while.

Allons! the inducements shall be greater,

We will sail pathless and wild seas,

We will go where winds blow, waves dash, and the Yankee
    clipper speeds by under full sail.

Allons! with power, liberty, the earth, the elements,

Health, defiance, gayety, self-esteem, curiosity;

Allons! from all formules! . . .

Camerado, I give you my hand!

I give you my love more precious than money,

I give you myself before preaching or law;

Will you give me yourself? will you come travel with me?

Shall we stick by each other as long as we live?

from "Song of the Open Road"

D. H. Lawrence

Do you think it is easy to change?
Ah, it is very hard to change and be different.
It means passing through the waters of oblivion.

"Change"

Are you willing to be sponged out, erased, cancelled,
made nothing?
Are you willing to be made nothing?
dipped into oblivion?

If not, you will never really change.

The phoenix renews her youth
only when she is burnt, burnt alive, burnt down
to hot and flocculent ash.
Then the small stirring of a new small bub in the nest
with strands of down like floating ash
Shows that she is renewing her youth like the eagle
Immortal bird.

"Phoenix"

Not every man has gentians in his house
in Soft September, at slow, sad Michaelmas.

Bavarian gentians, big and dark, only dark
darkening the day-time torch-like with the smoking blueness
    of Pluto's gloom,
ribbed and torch-like, with their blaze of darkness spread blue
down flattening into points, flattened under the sweep of white
    day

torch-flower of the blue-smoking darkness, Pluto's dark-blue
daze,
black lamps from the halls of Dio, burning dark blue,
giving off darkness, blue darkness, as Demeter's pale lamps
give off light,
lead me then, lead me the way.

Reach me a gentian, give me a torch!
let me guide myself with the blue, forked torch of this flower
down the darker and darker stairs, where blue is darkened on
blueness
even where Persephone goes, just now, from the frosted
September
to the sightless realm where darkness is awake upon the dark
and Persephone herself is but a voice
or a darkness invisible enfolded in the deeper dark
of the arms Plutonic, and pierced with the passion of dense
gloom,
among the splendour of torches of darkness, shedding darkness
on the lost bride and her groom.

"Bavarian Gentians"

God with honour hang your head,
Groom, and grace you, bride, your bed
With lissome scions, sweet scions,
Out of hallowed bodies bred.

Each be other's comfort kind:
Déep, déeper than divined,
Divine charity, dear charity,
Fast you ever, fast bind.

Then let the march tread our ears:
I to him turn with tears
Who to wedlock, his wonder wedlock,
Déals tríumph and immortal years.

GERARD MANLEY HOPKINS,
"At the Wedding March"

We have left the well-tracked beaches of proven facts and experiences. We are adventuring the chartless seas of imagination.

Is the golden fleece that awaits us some kind of new freedom for growth? And in this new freedom, is there any place for a relationship? I believe there is . . . an opportunity for the best relationship of all: not a limited, mutually exclusive one . . . and not a functional, dependent one . . . but the meeting of two whole fully developed people as persons. . . .

But this new relationship of persons as persons, this more human love, this two solitudes conception is not something that comes easily. . . . It cannot be reached until woman—individually and as a sex—has herself come of age, a maturing process we are witnessing today. In this undertaking she must work alone and cannot count on much help from the outsider, eager as he may be in pointing out the way. . . .

Woman must come of age by herself. This is the essence of "coming of age"—to learn how to stand alone. . . . She must find her true center alone. She must become whole. She must, it seems to me, as a prelude to any "two solitudes" relationship, follow the advice of the poet to become "world to oneself for another's sake."

In fact, I wonder if both man and woman must not accomplish this heroic feat. Must not man also become world to himself? Must he not also expand the neglected sides of his personality; the art of inward looking that he has seldom had time for in his active outward-going life; the personal relationships which he has not had as much chance to enjoy; the so-called feminine qualities, aesthetic, emotional, cultural and spiritual, which he has been too rushed to fully develop . . . ?

A good relationship has a pattern like a dance and is built on some of the same rules. The partners do not need to hold on tightly, because they move confidently in the same pattern, intricate but gay and swift and free, like a country dance of Mozart's. To touch heavily would be to arrest the pattern and freeze the movement, to check the endlessly changing beauty of its unfolding. There is no place here for the possessive clutch, the clinging arm, the heavy hand; only the barest touch in passing. Now arm in arm, now face to face, now back to back— it does not matter which. Because they know they are partners moving to the same rhythm, creating a pattern together, and being invisibly nourished by it.

The joy of such a pattern is not only the joy of creation or the joy of participation, it is also the joy of living in the moment. Lightness of touch and living in the moment are intertwined. One cannot dance well unless one is completely in time with

the music, not leaning back to the last step or pressing forward
to the next one, but poised directly on the present step as it
comes. Perfect poise on the beat is what gives good dancing
its sense of ease, of timelessness, of the eternal. . . .

ANNE MORROW LINDBERGH, from *Gift from the Sea*

We were on the pier, you desiring
That I see the Pleiades. I could see
everything but what you wished.

Now I will follow. There is not a single cloud; the stars
appear, even the invisible sister. Show me where to look,
as though they will stay where they are.

Instruct me in the dark.

LOUISE GLÜCK, "Under Taurus"

Corridors of the soul! The soul that is like a young woman!
You clear light
and the brief history
and the joy of a new life . . .

Oh turn and be born again, and walk the road,
and find once more the lost path!

. . . walk through life in dreams
out of love of the hand that leads us.

ANTONIO MACHADO, from "Rebirth,"
translation by Robert Bly

A change is taking place, some painful growth, as in a snake during the shedding of its skin. . . . It is difficult to adjust because I do not know who is adjusting; I am no longer that old person and not yet the new.

. . . With the past evaporated . . . I begin to experience that *now* that is spoken of by the great teachers.

To the repentant thief upon the cross, the soft Jesus of the modern Bible holds out hope of Heaven: "Today thou art with me in Paradise." But in older translations, there is no "today," no suggestion of the future. In the Russian translation, for example, the meaning is "right here now." Thus Jesus declares. "You are in Paradise right now" . . .

We climb onward, toward the sky, and with every step my spirits rise. . . . I begin to smile, infused with a sense of my own foolishness, with an acceptance of the failures of this journey as well as of its wonders, acceptance of all that I might meet upon my path. I know that this transcendence will be fleeting, but while it lasts, I spring along the path as if set free. . . .

PETER MATTHIESSEN, from *The Snow Leopard*

. . . Still, I am prepared for this voyage, and for anything else
    you may care to mention.
Not that I am afraid, but there is very little time left.
You have probably made travel arrangements, and know the
    feeling.
Suddenly, one morning, the little train arrives in the station,
    but oh, so big!

. . . Now we are both setting sail into the purplish evening.
I love it! This cruise can never last long enough for me.
. . . Ribbons are flung, ribbons of cloud

And the sun seems to be coming out. But there have been so
    many false alarms. . . .
No, it's happened! The storm is over. Again the weather is fine
    and clear. . . .

And the voyage? It's on! Listen everybody, the ship is starting,
I can hear its whistle's roar! We have just time enough to make
    it to the dock!

And away they pour, in the sulfurous sunlight,
To the aqua and silver waters where stands the glistening
    white ship
And into the great vessel they flood, a motley and happy crowd
Chanting and pouring down hymns on the surface of the
    ocean. . . .

Pulling, tugging us along with them, by means of streamers,
Golden and silver confetti. Smiling, we laugh and sing with
    the revelers
But are not quite certain that we want to go—the dock is so
    sunny and warm.
That majestic ship will pull up anchor who knows where?

And full of laughter and tears, we sidle once again with the
    other passengers.
The ground is heaving under foot. Is it the ship? It could
    be the dock. . . .
And with a great whoosh all the sails go up. . . .
. . . Into the secretive, vaporous night with all of us!
Into the unknown, the unknown that loves us, the great
    unknown!

JOHN ASHBERY, from "The Skaters"

Henceforth, from the mind,
For your whole joy, must spring
Such joy as you may find
In any earthly thing,
And every time and place
Will take your thought for grace.

Henceforth, from the tongue,
From shallow speech alone,
Comes joy you thought, when young,
Would wring you to the bone,
Would pierce you to the heart
And spoil its stop and star.

Henceforth, from the shell,
Wherein you heard, and wondered
At oceans like a bell
So far from ocean sundered—
A smothered sound that sleeps
Long lost within lost deeps,

Will chime you change and hours,
The shadow of increase,
Will sound you flowers
Born under troubled peace—
Henceforth, henceforth
Will echo sea and earth.

LOUISE BOGAN, "Henceforth, from the Mind"

"Come and play with me," proposed the little prince. "I am so unhappy."

"I cannot play with you," the fox said. "I am not tamed" . . .

"What does that mean, tame?"

"It is an act too often neglected," said the fox. "It means to establish ties . . . To me, you are still nothing more than a little boy who is just like a hundred thousand other little boys. And I have no need of you. And you, on your part, have no need of me. To you, I am nothing more than a fox like a hundred thousand other foxes. But if you tame me, then we shall need each other. To me, you will be unique in all the world. To you, I shall be unique in all the world . . .

"If you tame me, it will be as if the sun came to shine on my life. I shall know the sound of a step that will be different from all the others. Other steps send me hurrying back underneath the ground. Yours will call me, like music, out of my burrow . . . Think how wonderful that will be when you have tamed me! . . . One only understands the things that one tames . . . If you want a friend, tame me . . . "

"What must I do to tame you?" asked the little prince.

"You must be patient," replied the fox. "First you will sit down at a little distance from me—like that—in the grass. I shall look at you out of the corner of my eye, and you will say nothing. Words are the source of misunderstandings. But you will sit a little closer to me, every day . . . [and you must] come back at the same hour. If, for example, you come at four o'clock in the afternoon, then at three o'clock I shall begin to be happy. I shall feel happier and happier as the hour advances. At four o'clock I shall already be worrying and jumping about. I shall show you how happy I am! But if you come at just any time, I shall never know at what hour my heart is to be ready to greet you . . . One must observe the proper rites."

"What is a rite?" asked the prince.

"They are what make one day different from other days, one hour from other hours . . . "

So the prince tamed the fox . . .

[Then the little prince saw a garden of roses.] "You are not at all like *my* rose," he said. "As yet you are nothing. No one has tamed you, and you have tamed no one. You are like my fox when I first knew him. He was only a fox like a hundred thousand other foxes. But I have made him my friend, and now he is unique in all the world . . .

"You are beautiful, but you are empty," he went on. "One could not die for you. To be sure, an ordinary passerby would think that my rose looked just like you—the rose that belongs to me. But in herself alone she is more important than all the hundreds of you other roses: because it is she that I have watered . . . because it is she that I have sheltered . . . because it is she that I have listened to, when she grumbled, or boasted, or even sometimes when she said nothing. Because she is *my* rose."

And he went back to meet the fox.

"Goodbye," he said.

"Goodbye," said the fox. "And now here is my secret, a very simple secret: it is only with the heart that one can see rightly; what is essential is invisible to the eye . . .

"It is the time you have wasted for your rose that makes your rose so important . . .

"You become responsible, forever, for what you have tamed. You are responsible for your rose."

Antoine de Saint-Exupéry, from *The Little Prince*,
translation by Katherine Woods

IV

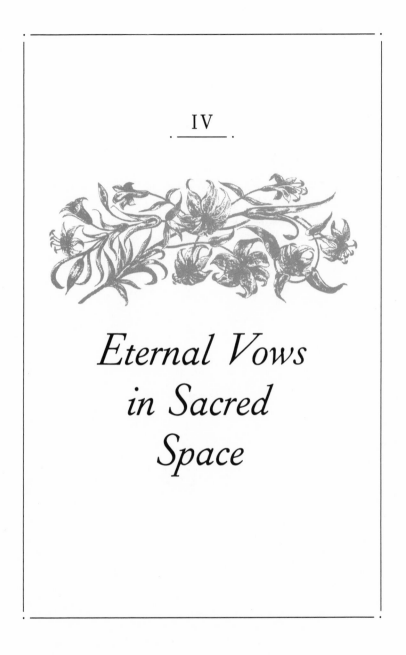

Eternal Vows
in Sacred
Space

Tonight is a night of *union* and also of scattering of the stars,
for a bride is coming from the sky: the full moon.
The sky is an astrolabe, and the Law is Love.

JALAL AL-DIN RUMI, Persian love poem,
translation by A. J. Arberry

*T*he marriage ceremony itself may be short but it should set the course of the couple's life to come, drawing them into the community in which, like their parents before them, they'll play thereafter a generative role. The event takes place in a sanctuary of sacred space, which is also, in certain religious systems, to be imagined as a place of stopped time. There the celebrant of each religion explains the mysteries and responsibilities of human union, its social, theological, and even metaphysical implications. In Jewish custom, a canopy held over the bridal couple marks the plot as a corner of Eden, a sign of continuity between the world of the Torah and today. In Christian, Hindu, and Buddhist custom, ministers and priests may call down benedictions on the new couple from divine presences beyond the moment. Secular weddings also take place in the presence of symbols and icons—flags, a national seal, accreditation documents of the presiding official (a notary public, a ship's captain), certain features of landscape, and so forth. Even for people whose religious ideas are perfunctory, exchange of wedding vows is no trivial event but should be understood as integrative of life on a deep level.

In fact the human family has evolved countless variations on the rites of union, documented in detail by anthropologists of the nineteenth and early twentieth centuries. I have included short excerpts from two of these standard texts to give an idea of their breadth. Some of this information and some of the liturgical passages included here may strike one as odd. Yet they are all rooted in common traditions of myth and belief, and similar notions resonate through world poetry.

The Marriage of the Gods: At Babylon the imposing sanctuary of Bel rose like a pyramid above the city in a series of eight towers or stories, planted one on the top of the other. On the highest tower, reached by an ascent which wound about all the rest, there stood a spacious temple, and in the temple a great bed, magnificently draped and cushioned, with a golden table beside it. In the temple no image was to be seen, and no human being passed the night there, save a single woman, whom, according to the Chaldean priests, the god chose from among all the women of Babylon. They said that the deity himself came into the temple at night and slept in the great bed; and the woman, as a consort of the god, might have no intercourse with mortal man.

At Thebes in Egypt a woman slept in the temple of Ammon as the consort of the god, and, like the human wife of Bel at Babylon, she was said to have no commerce with a man. . . .

At Athens the god of the vine, Dionysus, was annually married to the Queen, and it appears that the consummation of the divine union, as well as the espousals, was enacted at the ceremony; but whether the part of the god was played by a man or an image we do not know. . . . The object of the marriage can hardly have been any other than that of ensuring the fertility of the vines and other fruit-trees of which Dionysus was the god. Thus both in form and in meaning the ceremony would answer to the nuptials of the King and Queen of May.

In the great mysteries solemnised at Eleusis in the month of September the union of the sky-god Zeus with the corn-goddess Demeter appears to have been represented by the union of the hierophant with the priestess of Demeter, who acted the parts of god and goddess. . . . Thus the custom of marrying gods either to images or to human beings was widespread among the nations of antiquity.

SIR JAMES GEORGE FRAZER,
from *The Golden Bough: A Study in Magic and Religion*

Marriage being the permanent living-together of a man and a woman, what is the essence of a marriage ceremony? It is the "joining together" of a man and a woman; in the words of the English Service, "for this cause shall a man leave his father and mother and shall be joined unto his wife; and they two shall be one flesh." At the other side of the world, these words are pronounced by an elder [of the Malacca Straits] when a marriage is solemnised: "Listen all ye that are present; those that were distant are now brought together; those that were separated are now united." Before marriage, and in many cases also after marriage, the sexes are separated by ideas of sexual taboo; at marriage, they are joined together by the same ideas. Those who were separated are now joined together, those who were mutually taboo, now break the taboo. It is unnecessary to re-capitulate the various dangers responsible for the taboo, which lead to the idea that not only all contact of man and woman but the state of marriage itself is harmful and, later, sinful, in fact, forbidden. Hence, the conception that marriage ceremonies prevent this danger and this sin. We have, however, seen cases where the individual in marriage is consciously aware that it is his human partner who is to be feared. In [Ireland] men with guns used to escort the bridal party to church. The guns were fired at intervals over the heads of the bride and bridesmaids. The same practice of firing over the heads of bride and bridegroom on the way to or from the church in which the marriage ceremony is celebrated is found in many parts of Europe. Amongst the Mordvins, as the bridegroom's party sets out for the house of the bride, the best man marches thrice round the party with a drawn sword or scythe, imprecating curses upon ill-wishers. In Nizhegorod the best man walks thrice round the party, against the sun, holding an *ikon*. Then he places himself in front of them, and scratches the ground with a knife, cursing evil spirits and evilly disposed persons. . . .

The practice of throwing rice originated in the idea of giving food to the evil influences to induce them to be propitious and depart, but in many cases it seems to have developed into a systematic method of securing fertility, and on the other hand is regarded by some peoples as an inducement to the soul to stay. In Celebes, for instance, there is a belief that the bridegroom's soul is apt to fly away at marriage, and rice is therefore scattered over him to induce it to remain. . . .

A common class of preliminary ceremonial includes various kinds of purification, the inner meaning of which is to neutralise the mutual dangers of contact. Before the wedding the bridegroom in South Celebes bathes in holy water. The bride is also fumigated. Purification by water forms an integral part of Malay customs at birth, adolescence, marriage, sickness, death, and, in fact, at every critical period in the life of a Malay. The first ceremonies at a wedding consist in fumigating the bride and groom with incense, and then smearing them with "neutralising paste" which averts ill-luck.

Weddings very commonly take place in the evening, or at night, a custom natural enough for its convenience and its obviation of dangers, such as that of the evil eye and those connected with human, and especially with female, shyness and timidity. Amongst the Santals marriages take place at night, and the bride is conveyed to her husband in a basket. Amongst the ancient Romans the bridegroom had to go to his bride in the dark, a custom on which Plutarch speculates in his Roman Questions. Amongst the Zulus it is against etiquette for the bridal party to enter the bridegroom's hut in the daytime. . . .

There are some interesting customs which show both the taboo character of bride and bridegroom, and also an attempt at disguising them by fictitious change of identity. The Malay wedding ceremony, even as carried out by the poorer classes, shows that the contracting parties are treated as royalty, that is to say, as sacred human beings. During the first week of marriage the Syrian pair play at being king and queen; they sit on a throne, and the villagers sing songs. It has been conjectured that *The Song of Songs* is a collection of such songs.

Somewhat similar is the idea underlying the habit of wearing finery or new clothes for a new or important event. On the same plane is the common custom of erecting a "marriage-bower," well known amongst the Hindu peoples, and once common in Spain. In the mining districts of Fife, when a bridal company set out in procession for the kirk, the bride and bridegroom were sometimes "bowered," that is, an arch of green boughs was held over their heads.

Next comes the very interesting custom of substituting a mock bride for the real one. Thus amongst the Beni-Amer, the groom and his friends are often mocked when they come to take the bride, her people substituting a false bride for the true one. The substitute is carefully disguised and allows herself to be taken, and at last when the procession is well outside the village, she reveals herself and runs back laughing. Amongst the Saxons of Transylvania, the bride is concealed with two married women behind a curtain, on the evening of the wedding-day, and the husband has to guess which is his wife, all three try to mislead him. Amongst the Moksha, an old woman dressed up as a bride danced before the company. Amongst the Esthonians, the bride's brother dresses up in women's clothes and personates the bride. In Brittany, the substitutes are first a little girl, then the mistress of the house, and lastly the grandmother.

We now reach the ceremonies which, more than any others, unite the man and the woman. Each of the two parties gives to the other a part of himself and receives from the other a part of him; this part, on the principles of contact, may be, as it is in love-charms, a lock of hair, a piece of clothing, food that has or has not been touched, blood, and the like. This effects union by assimilating the one to the other, so as to produce somewhat of identity of substance. . . .

The commonest of all marriage ceremonies of union is eating and drinking together. This breaks the most important of sexual taboos, that against eating together. The offering of a gift of food, which is part of the biological basis of the custom, is often used as a proposal of marriage. In Halmahera and Borneo a proposal is made by offering *betel* to the girl. She shows her acceptance by receiving it. In Samoa the suitor offers her a basket of bread-fruit; or he asks her parents for her hand. If they are friendly and eat with him, his addresses are sure to be favourably received. In Switzerland, if a youth and a girl fall in love, on the Easter Monday after, they publicly drink together in order to inform the world at large of their love and to warn off others who might wish to approach the girl. . . . In the Duke of York Islands a cocoanut is broken over the heads of the pair, and its milk poured over them. Amongst the Koosa Kaffirs the relatives of the groom hand milk to the bride, reminding her that it is from the cows which belong to the bridegroom. Of this milk she may not drink while the bridegroom is her suitor only, but now she is to drink it, and from this moment the union is indissolubly concluded. The people shout, "She drinks the milk! She hath drunk the milk!" . . .

The survey of marriage suggests many thoughts. For instance, one is struck by the high morality of [early] man. The religious character of early human relations, again, gives a sense of tragedy: man seems to feel that he is treading in slippery places, that he is on the brink of precipices, when really he standeth right. This sensitive attitude would seem to have assisted the natural development of man. . . . Lastly, this desire for security and permanence in a world where only change is permanent has led to certain conceptions of eternal personalities who control and symbolise the marriage tie . . . [for example] the Goddess of Love . . . the Holy Family . . . the eternal feminine . . . the Mystical Rose.

ERNEST CRAWLEY, from *The Mystic Rose: A Study of Primitive Marriage and of Primitive Thought in Its Bearing on Marriage*

Therefore must the bride below have a canopy, all beautiful with decorations prepared for her, in order to honor the Bride above, who comes to be present and participate in the joy of the bride below. For this reason it is necessary that the canopy be as beautiful as possible, and that the Supernal Bride be invited to come and share in the joy.

from "Terumah," in the *Zohar*

The chuppah stands on four poles.
The home has four corners.
The chuppah stands on four poles.

The marriage stands on four legs.
Four points loose the winds
that blow on the walls of the house,

the south wind that brings the warm rain,
the east wind that brings the cold rain,
the north wind that brings the cold sun
and the snow, the long west wind
bringing the weather off the far plains.

Here we live open to the seasons.
Here the winds caress and cuff us
contrary and fierce as bears.
Here the winds are caught and snarling
in the pines, a cat in a net clawing
breaking twigs to fight loose.
Here the winds brush your face
soft in the morning as feathers
that float down from the dove's breast.

Here the moon sails up out of the ocean
dripping like a just washed apple.
Here the sun wakes us like a baby.
Therefore the chuppah has no sides.

It is not a box.
It is not a coffin.
It is not a dead end.
Therefore the chuppah has no walls.
We have made a home together
open to the weather of our time.
We are mills that turn in the winds of struggle
converting fierce energy into bread.

The canopy is the cloth of our table
where we share fruit and vegetables
of our labor, where our care for the earth
comes back and we take its body in ours.

The canopy is the cover of our bed
where our bodies open their portals wide,
where we eat and drink the blood
of our love, where the skin shines red
as a swallowed sunrise and we burn
in one furnace of joy molten as steel
and the dream is fresh and flower.

O my love O my love we dance
under the chuppah standing over us
like an animal on its four legs,
like a table on which we set our love
as a feast, like a tent
under which we work
not safe but no longer solitary
in the searing heat of our time.

MARGE PIERCY, "The Chuppah,"
June 2, 1982, on her marriage to Ira Wood

Blessed are you, Holy One of the Earth, who creates
the fruit of the vine.
Blessed are you, Holy One of the Universe. You
created all things for your Glory.
Blessed are you, Holy One of the World.
Through you mankind lives.
Blessed are you, Holy One of the World. You made
man and woman in your image, after your likeness, that
they might perpetuate life. . . .
Blessed are you, Holy One of All Nature, who makes
Zion rejoice with her children. . . .
Blessed are you, Holy One of the Cosmos, who makes
the bridegroom and bride to rejoice.

Blessed are you, Holy One of All, who created joy
and gladness, bride and bridegroom, mirth and song,
pleasure and delight, love, fellowship, peace
and friendship. . . .

The Hebrew "Seven Blessings"

In the sixteenth century the kabbalists of Safed personified the
Sabbath as a bride and welcomed her every week with fervent
joy. These mystics would go forth to the hills surrounding the
city, robed in white as grooms and would greet the incoming
Sabbath with the chanting of *Lekhah Dodi*—"Come, my friend,
to greet the bride, to receive the presence of the Sabbath." This
well-known hymn, composed by Rabbi Solomon Halevi Alk-
abetz, is still sung at Friday evening services. The celebration
of the Sabbath was considered a wedding feast.

In talmudic days Rabbi Yanni would don his Sabbath clothes
on Friday before evening and say: "Come, O bride, come, O
bride."

PHILIP and HANNA GOODMAN, "The Sabbath as Bride"

Come my beloved, with chorus of praise,
Welcome Bride Sabbath, the Queen of the days . . .
Come in thy joyousness, Crown of thy lord;
Come, bringing peace to the folk of the Word;
Come where the faithful in gladsome accord,
    Hail thee as Sabbath-Bride, Queen of the days.
Come where the faithful are hymning thy praise,
Come as a bride cometh, Queen of the days!

from "Lekhah Dodi," Hebrew hymn to the Sabbath as a bride

Psalms

O sing unto the Lord a new song; for he hath done marvellous things: . . .

4 Make a joyful noise unto the Lord, all the earth: make a loud noise, and rejoice, and sing praise.

5 Sing unto the Lord with the harp; with the harp, and the voice of a psalm.

6 With trumpets and sound of cornets make a joyful noise before the Lord, the King.

7 Let the sea roar, and the fulness thereof; the world, and they that dwell therein.

8 Let the floods clap their hands: let the hills be joyful together

9 Before the Lord. . . .

PSALM 100

Make a joyful noise unto the Lord, all ye lands.

2 Serve the Lord with gladness: come before his presence with singing.

3 Know ye that the Lord he is God: it is he that hath made us, and not we ourselves; we are his people, and the sheep of his pasture.

4 Enter into his gates with thanksgiving, and into his courts with praise: be thankful unto him, and bless his name.

5 For the Lord is good, his mercy is everlasting, and his truth endureth to all generations.

Bless the Lord, O my soul. O Lord my God, thou art very great; thou art clothed with honour and majesty.

2 Who coverest thyself with light as with a garment: who stretchest out the heavens like a curtain:

3 Who layeth the beams of his chambers in the waters: who maketh the clouds his chariot: who walketh upon the wings of the wind:

4 Who maketh his angels spirits; his ministers a flaming fire:

5 Who laid the foundations of the earth, that it should not be removed for ever.

6 Thou coveredst it with the deep as with a garment: the waters stood above the mountains.

7 At thy rebuke they fled; at the voice of thy thunder they hasted away.

8 They go up by the mountains; they go down by the valleys unto the place which thou hast founded for them.

9 Thou hast set a bound that they may not pass over; that they turn not again to cover the earth.

10 He sendeth the springs into the valleys, which run among the hills.

11 They give drink to every beast of the field: the wild asses quench their thirst.

12 By them shall the fowls of the heaven have their habitation, which sing among the branches.

13 He watereth the hills from his chambers: the earth is satisfied with the fruit of thy works.

14 He causeth the grass to grow for the cattle, and herb for the service of man: that he may bring forth food out of the earth;

15 And wine that maketh glad the heart of man, and oil to

make his face to shine, and bread which strengtheneth man's
heart.

16 The trees of the Lord are full of sap; the cedars of Lebanon, which he hath planted;

17 Where the birds make their nests; as for the stork, the fir
trees are her house.

18 The high hills are a refuge for the wild goats; and the
rocks for the conies.

19 He appointed the moon for seasons: the sun knoweth his
going down.

20 Thou makest darkness and it is night: wherein all the
beasts of the forest do creep forth.

21 The young lions roar after their prey, and seek their meat
from God.

22 The sun ariseth, they gather themselves together, and lay
them down in their dens.

23 Man goeth forth unto his work and to his labour until
the evening.

24 O Lord, how manifold are thy works! in wisdom hast
thou made them all: the earth is full of thy riches.

25 So is this great and wide sea, wherein are things creeping
innumerable, both small and great beasts.

26 There go the ships: there is that leviathan, whom thou
hast made to play therein.

27 These wait all upon thee; that thou mayest give them
their meat in due season.

28 That thou givest them they gather: thou openest thine
hand, they are filled with good.

29 Thou hidest thy face, they are troubled: thou takest away
their breath, they die, and return to their dust.

30 Thou sendest forth thy spirit, they are created: and thou
renewest the face of the earth.

31 The glory of the Lord shall endure for ever: the Lord shall rejoice in his works.

32 He looketh on the earth, and it trembleth: he toucheth the hills, and they smoke.

33 I will sing unto the Lord as long as I live: I will sing praise to my God while I have my being.

34 My meditation of him shall be sweet: I will be glad in the Lord . . .

(King James Version)

Blessed be You, Life-Spirit of the universe,
Who makes a distinction between holy and not yet
    holy,
between light and darkness,
between Shabbat and the six days of the week,
between committed and uncommitted,
between common goals and personal goals,
between love and aloneness.
Blessed be you,
Who distinguishes between what is holy, and what is
    not yet holy.

Hebrew blessing for Sabbath end

Rejoice, O young man, in thy youth,
　　And gather the fruit thy joy shall bear,
Thou and the wife of thy youth,
　　Turning now to thy dwelling to enter there.

Glorious blessings of God, who is One,
　　Shall come united upon thine head;
　　Thine house shall be at peace from dread,
Thy foes' uprising be undone.
　　Thou shalt lay thee down in a safe retreat;
　　Thou shalt rest, and thy sleep be sweet.

In thine honor, my bridegroom, prosper and live;
　　Let thy beauty arise and shine forth fierce;
　　And the heart of thine enemies God shall pierce,
And the sins of thy youth will He forgive,
　　And bless thee in increase and all thou shalt do.
　　When thou settest thine hand thereto. . . .

JUDAH HALEVI, from a poem to the bridegroom,
translation by Nina Davis

Thus saith the Lord; Again there shall be heard in this place
. . . The voice of joy, and the voice of gladness, the voice of
the bridegroom, and the voice of the bride, the voice of them
that shall say, Praise the Lord of hosts: for the Lord is good:
for his mercy endureth for ever.

Jeremiah 33:10–11 (King James Version)

Dearly beloved: We have come together in the presence of God
to witness and bless the joining together of this man and this
woman in Holy Matrimony. The bond and covenant of marriage
was established by God in creation, and our Lord Jesus Christ

adorned this manner of life by his presence and first miracle at a wedding in Cana of Galilee. It signifies to us the mystery of the union between Christ and his Church, and Holy Scripture commends it to be honored among all people.

The union of husband and wife in heart, body, and mind is intended by God for their mutual joy; for the help and comfort given one another in prosperity and adversity; and, when it is God's will, for the procreation of children and their nurture in the knowledge and love of the Lord. Therefore marriage is not to be entered into unadvisedly or lightly, but reverently, deliberately, and in accordance with the purposes for which it was instituted by God.

from "The Celebration and Blessing of a Marriage,"
in *The Book of Common Prayer* (Episcopal)

Eternal God, creator and preserver of all life, author of salvation, and giver of all grace: Look with favor upon the world you have made, and for which your Son gave his life, and especially upon this man and this woman whom you make one flesh in Holy Matrimony.

Give them wisdom and devotion in the ordering of their common life, that each may be to the other a strength in need, a counselor in perplexity, a comfort in sorrow, and a companion in joy.

Grant that their wills may be so knit together in your will, and their spirits in your Spirit, that they may grow in love and peace with you and one another all the days of their life.

Give them grace, when they hurt each other, to recognize and acknowledge their fault, and to seek each other's forgiveness and yours.

Make their life together a sign of Christ's love to this sinful and broken world, that unity may overcome estrangement, forgiveness heal guilt, and joy conquer despair.

Bestow on them, if it is your will, the gift and heritage of children, and the grace to bring them up to know you, to love you, and to serve you.

Give them such fulfillment of their mutual affection that they may reach out in love and concern for others.

Grant that all married persons who have witnessed these vows may find their lives strengthened and their loyalties confirmed.

Grant that the bonds of our common humanity, by which all your children are united one to another, and the living to the dead, may be so transformed by your grace, that your will may be done on earth as it is in heaven; where, O Father, with your Son and the Holy Spirit, you live and reign in perfect unity, now and for ever.

from *The Book of Common Prayer*

The maiden is the daughter of light . . .
Delightful is the sight of her,
Radiant with shining beauty.
Her garments are like spring flowers,
And a scent of sweet fragrance is diffused from them . . .
Truth rests upon her head.
By the movements of her feet, she shows forth joy . . .
Her two hands make signs and secret patterns, describing the dance of the blessed aeons.
Her fingers open the gates of the city.
Her chamber is full of light . . .
Her bridesmaids are seven,
Who dance before her.

Twelve are they who serve her
And are subject to her,
Gazing toward the bridegroom
That by the sight of him they may be enlightened;
And forever be with him in eternal joy.
Bride and groom shall be at that marriage . . .
And both shall be in joy and exultation.
And thus they glorified and praised, with the living Spirit,
The Father of Truth and the Mother of Wisdom.

from the apocryphal Acts of Thomas, translation by R. McL. Wilson

Husbands, love your wives as you love your own bodies. In loving his wife a man loves himself. For no one ever hated his own body: on the contrary, he provides and cares for it; and thus it is that a man shall leave his father and mother and shall be joined to his wife and the two shall become one flesh.

It is a great truth that is hidden here . . .

Ephesians 4:25–32 (New English Bible)

Have you not read that he who made them from the beginning made them male and female, and said, "For this reason a man shall leave his father and mother and be joined to his wife, and the two shall become one"? So they are no longer two but one. What therefore God has joined together, let no man put asunder.

Matthew 19:4–6 (New English Bible)

Beloved, let us love one another; for love is of God, and he who loves is born of God and knows God. He who does not love does not know God; for God is love. . . . Beloved, if God so loved us, we also ought to love one another. No man has ever seen God; if we love one another, God abides in us and his love is perfected in us.

1 John 4:7–12 (New English Bible)

Put on then, as God's chosen ones, holy and beloved, compassion, kindness, lowliness, meekness, and patience, forbearing one another and, if one has a complaint against another, forgiving each other; as the Lord has forgiven you, so you also must forgive. And above all these put on love, which binds everything together in perfect harmony. And let peace rule in your hearts . . . And be thankful. Let love dwell in you richly, as you teach and admonish one another in all wisdom . . .

Colossians 3:12–17 (New English Bible)

Be thou magnified, O bridegroom, like Abraham, and blessed like Isaac, and increase like Jacob, walking in peace and living in righteousness . . .

And thou, O bride, be magnified like Sarah, and rejoice like Rebecca, and increase like Rachel, being glad in thy husband and keeping the bounds of the law . . .

from the Greek Orthodox marriage service

We thank thee, O Lord God almighty, who art before the ages, master of the universe, who didst adorn the heavens by thy word, and didst lay the foundations of the earth and all that is therein; who didst gather together those things which were separate into union, and didst make the twain one. Now again, our Master, we beseech thee, may thy servants be worthy of the mark of the sign of thy Word through the bond of betrothal, their love for one another inviolable through the firm sureness of their union. Build them, O Lord, upon the foundation of thy holy Church, that they may walk in accordance with the bond of the word which they have vowed one to another; for thou art the bond of their love, and the ordainer of the law of their union. Thou who hast brought about the oneness, by the union of the twain by thy words, cómplete, O Lord, the ordinance of thine only-begotten Son Jesus Christ our Lord, through whom and together with the all-Holy Spirit be praise to thee now and always.

from the Coptic Orthodox marriage service

We have taken the seven steps. You have become mine forever. Yes, we have become partners. I have become yours. Hereafter, I cannot live without you. Do not live without me. Let us share the joys. We are word and meaning, united. You are thought and I am sound.

May the nights be honey-sweet for us; may the mornings be honey-sweet for us; may the earth be honey-sweet for us; may the heavens be honey-sweet for us.

May the plants be honey-sweet for us; may the sun be all honey for us; may the cows yield us honey-sweet milk!

As the heavens are stable, as the earth is stable, as the mountains are stable, as the whole universe is stable, so may our union be permanently settled.

from the Hindu marriage ritual of "Seven Steps"

O Lord Fire, First Created Being! Be thou the over-lord and give food and drink to this household. O Lord Fire, who reigns in richness and vitality over all the worlds, come take your proper seat in this home! Accept the offerings made here, protect the one who makes them, be our protector on this day, O you who see into the hearts of all created beings!

Hindu wedding prayer

Nothing happens without a cause. The union of this man and woman has not come about accidentally but is the foreordained result of many past lives. This tie can therefore not be broken or dissolved.

In the future, happy occasions will come as surely as the morning. Difficult times will come as surely as night. When things go joyously, meditate according to the Buddhist tradition. When things go badly, meditate. Meditation in the manner of the Compassionate Buddha will guide your life.

To say the words "love and compassion" is easy. But to accept that love and compassion are built upon patience and perseverance is not easy. Your marriage will be firm and lasting if you remember this.

Buddhist marriage homily

Wash your hearts and souls clean of dust in the water of Wisdom so you won't have regrets. Isn't it always the case that Love is the essence? Apart from Love, everything passes away.

The way to heaven is in your heart. Open and lift the wings of Love! When Love's wings are strong, you need no ladder.

Though the world be thorns, a lover's heart is a bower of roses.

Though heaven's wheel be mired down, lovers' lives go
    forward.
Let other people be downcast, the lover is blissful and sprightly.
Invite a lover into each dark corner. The lover is bright as a
    hundred thousand candles!
Even if a lover seems to be alone, the secret Beloved is nearby.

The wind of ignorance has died down; the wind of love has
    risen. The heart puts forth roses, eglantine and basil,
    watered by the rain of generosity.

The time-span of *union* is eternity.
This life is a jar, and in it, *union* is the pure wine.
If we aren't togther, of what use is the jar?

The moment I heard my first love story I began seeking you,
not realizing the search was useless.
Lovers don't meet somewhere along the way.
They're in one another's souls from the beginning.

You are the sea, I am a fish . . .

I am a crystal goblet in my Love's hand.
Look into my eyes if you don't believe me.

JALAL AL-DIN RUMI, Persian love poem,
adapted from the translation by A. J. Arberry

Julia, I bring
To thee this ring,
    Made for thy finger fit;
To show by this
That our love is
    Or should be, like to it.

Loose though it be,
The joint is free;
    So, when love's yoke is on,
It must not gall,
Nor fret at all,
    With hard oppression.

But it must play,
Still either way,
    And be, too, such a yoke
As not too wide
To overslide,
    Or be so straight to choke.

So we who bear
This beam, must rear
    Ourselves to such a height
As that the stay
Of either may
    Create the burthen light.

And as this round
Is nowhere found
    To flaw, or else to sever,
So let our love
As endless prove,
    And pure as gold forever.

ROBERT HERRICK, "To Julia"

Go little ring to that same sweet
That hath my heart in her domain . . .

GEOFFREY CHAUCER

Open the temple gates unto my love,
Open them wide that she may enter in,
And all the posts adorn as doth behove,
And all the pillars deck with garlands trim,
For to receive this saint with honour due,
That cometh in to you . . .

Bring her up to the high altar, that she may
The sacred ceremonies there partake,
The which do endless matrimony make;
And let the roaring organ loudly play
The praises of the Lord in lively notes;
The whiles, with hollow throats,
The choristers the joyous anthem sing,
That all the woods may answer, and their echoes ring. . . .

Sing, ye sweet angels, Alleluia sing,
That all the woods may answer and your echo ring.

EDMUND SPENSER, from "Epithalamion"

Hear the mellow wedding bells,—
Golden bells!
What a world of happiness their harmony foretells!
Through the balmy air of night
How they ring out their delight!
From the molten golden notes,
What a liquid ditty floats
To the turtle-dove that listens, while she gloats
On the moon!
Oh, from out the sounding cells,
What a gush of euphony voluminously wells!
How it swells!
How it dwells

On the Future! How it tells
Of the rapture that impels
To the swinging and the ringing
Of the bells, bells, bells,
Of the bells, bells, bells, bells,
Bells, bells, bells,—
To the rhyming and the chiming of the bells!

EDGAR ALLAN POE, from "The Bells"

When our two souls stand up erect and strong,
Face to face, silent, drawing nigh and nigher,
Until the lengthening wings break into fire
At either curved point,—what bitter wrong
Can the earth do us, that we should not long
Be here contented! Think. In mounting higher,
The angels would press on us and aspire
To drop some golden orb of perfect song
Into our deep, dear silence. Let us stay
Rather on earth, Beloved—where the unfit
Contrarious moods of men recoil away
And isolate pure spirits, and permit
A place to stand and love in for a day . . .

ELIZABETH BARRETT BROWNING, from Sonnet XXII
from Sonnets from the Portuguese

That I may come near to her, draw me nearer to thee than to
her; that I may know her, make me to know thee more than
her; that I may love her with the perfect love of a perfectly
whole heart, cause me to love thee more than her and most of
all. Amen. Amen.

That nothing may be between me and her, be thou between us, every moment. That we may be constantly togther, draw us into separate loneliness with thyself. And when we meet breast to breast, my God, let it be on thine own. Amen. Amen.

TEMPLE GAIRDNER, prayer before his marriage

He is here, Urania's son,
Hymen come, from helicon;
God that glads the lover's heart,
He is here to join and part.
So the groomsman quits your side
And the bridegroom seeks the bride:
Friend and comrade yield you o'er
To her that hardly loves you more.

Now the sun his skyward beam
Hast tilted from the Ocean stream.
Light the Indies, laggard sun:
Happy bridegroom, day is done,
And the star from Oeta's steep
Calls to bed but not to sleep.

Happy bridegroom, Hesper brings
All desired and timely things.
All whom morning sends to roam,
Hesper loves to lead them home.
Home return who him behold,
Child to mother, sheep to fold,
Bird to nest from wandering wide:
Happy bridegroom, seek your bride.

Pour it out, the golden cup
Given and guarded, brimming up,
Safe through jostling markets borne
And the thicket of the thorn;
Folly spured and danger past,
Pour it to the god at last.

Now, to smother noise and light,
Is stolen abroad the wildering night,
And the blotting shades confuse
Path and meadow full of dews;
And the high heavens, that all control,
Turn in silence round the pole.
Catch the starry beams they shed
Prospering the marriage bed.

. . . All is quiet, no alarms;
Nothing fear of nightly harms.
Safe you sleep on guarded ground,
And in silent circle round
The thoughts of friends keep watch and ward,
Harnessed angels, hand on sword.

A. E. Housman, from "Epithalamium"

". . . I hereby give myself. I love you. You are the only being whom I can love absolutely with my complete self, with all my flesh and mind and heart. You are my mate, my perfect partner, and I am yours. You must *feel* this now, as I do. . . . It was a marvel that we ever met. It is some kind of divine luck that we are together now. We must never, never part again. We are, here in this, *necessary* beings, like gods. As we look at each other we verify, we *know*, the perfection of our love, we *recognise* each other. *Here* is my life, here if need be is my death. It's life and death, as if they were to destroy Israel—if I forget thee, O Jerusalem—"

Iris Murdoch, from *The Book and the Brotherhood*

. . . may her bridegroom bring her to a house
Where all's accustomed, ceremonious;
For arrogance and hatred are the wares
Peddled in the thoroughfares.
How but in custom and in ceremony
Are innocence and beauty born?
Ceremony's a name for the rich horn,
And custom for the spreading laurel tree.

William Butler Yeats,
from "A Prayer for My Daughter"

To the wife of my bosom
All happiness from everything
And her husband.
May he be good and considerate
Gay and cheerful and restful.
And make her the best wife
In the world
The happiest and the most content
With reason.
To the wife of my bosom
Whose transcendent virtues
Are those to be most admired
Loved and adored and indeed
Her virtues are all inclusive

Her virtues her beauty and her beauties
Her charms her qualities her joyous nature
All of it makes of her husband
A proud and happy man . . .

GERTRUDE STEIN, from "Patriarchal Poetry"

V

The Miracle of
the Body

I'm the one who has the body,
you're the one who holds the breath.

You know the secret of my body,
I know the secret of your breath.

That's why your body
is in mine.

You know
and I know, Ramanatha,

the miracle

of your breath
in my body.

Devara Dasimayya,
poem to Lord Siva (Ramanatha),
translation by A. K. Ramanujan

*T*he sexual revolution and the development of birth control have changed the pattern of life for many couples in the Western world, but wedding ceremonies still contain veiled celebrations of the act of sexual initiation.

Some passages in the section that follows may be inappropriate for reading aloud in a formal setting. But wise men and women, as all soon-to-be-married couples must be, know we live in this life in our bodies, which inspire in us the love we may later on choose to celebrate in its transcendent aspects. We go as desire moves us: the poet Denise Levertov calls it "the ache of marriage . . . the ark of the ache of it."

Hail to Priapus, father of us all, hail!
Grant me eternally flowering virility
So I may charm both men and beautiful girls.
Keep me from being worn out by tedious
dinner parties and festivals,
And don't send me old age, decrepitude, or some unhappy death
Which will drag me off to the land
from where no one returns.
Hail to holy Priapus, father Priapus, hail!
Up and away, O joyous throng,
However many you are,
Up and away, run!
Run to the sacred wood,
You maidens who worship the sacred waters,
Run, all of you, to friendly Priapus,
And say in your charming voices:
Hail, O holy Priapus, father of us all, hail!
In fact, it is he who bids us sport in the woods,
Frolic in the water as we like.
He keeps bothersome people at a distance,
Those who irreverently pollute the streams.
So now say to him:
O Priapus, O divine one, be good to us!
O Priapus, powerful friend, hail,
And may it please you to be called

Progenitor of the whole world,
Yes, even of the Universe itself, even of Pan!
For in truth, earth, air, and sea were conceived
Out of your virility, your vigorous lust.
Jove himself lays down his thunderbolts when you speak,
While lovely Venus honors you, and Cupid does too,
And Grace, with her dancing sisters,
Bringers of joy, while
Virgins call on you to prepare them for marriage and
The bride calls on you to make sure
Her husband's manhood will stand shining forever.
Hail, O sacred father Priapus, hail!

Greek Prayer to Priapus

O Bride brimful of
rosy little loves!

O brightest jewel of
the Queen of Paphos!

Come now
        to your
bedroom to your
bed
    and play there
sweetly   gently
with your bridegroom

And may Hesperus
lead you not at all
unwilling
        until

you stand wondering
before the silver

Throne of Hera
Queen of Marriage

SAPPHO, translation
by Mary Barnard

249

Wild Nights - Wild Nights!
Were I with thee
Wild Nights should be
Our luxury!

Futile - the Winds -
To a Heart in port -
Done with the Compass -
Done with the Chart!

Rowing in Eden -
Ah, the Sea!
Might I but moor - Tonight -
In Thee!

EMILY DICKINSON,
from *The Complete Poems*,
edited by Thomas H. Johnson

I know not whether thou has been absent:
I lie down with thee, I rise up with thee,
In my dreams thou art with me.
If my eardrops tremble in my ears,
I know it is thou moving within my heart.

Aztec love song

The Song of
Solomon

Characters:

KING SOLOMON
THE SHULAMITE
THE BROTHERS
CHORUS OF THE DAUGHTERS OF JERUSALEM

Scene I

THE SHULAMITE (the bride)

Let him kiss me with the kisses of his mouth:
For thy love is better than wine.

The king hath brought me into his chambers.

THE DAUGHTERS OF JERUSALEM

We will be glad and rejoice in thee,
We will make mention of thy love more than of wine:
Rightly do they love thee.

THE SHULAMITE

I am black, but comely,
O ye daughters of Jerusalem,
As the tents of Kedar,
As the curtains of Solomon.

Look not upon me, because I am swarthy,
Because the sun hath scorched me.

Tell me, O thou whom my soul loveth,
Where thou feedest thy flock, where thou makest it to rest at
    noon:
For why should I be as one that is veiled
Beside the flocks of thy companions?

KING SOLOMON

If thou know not, O thou fairest among women,
Go thy way forth by the footsteps of the flock,
And feed thy kids beside the shepherds' tents.

I have compared thee, O my love,
To a steed in Pharaoh's chariots.
Thy cheeks are comely with plaits of hair,
Thy neck with strings of jewels.
We will make thee plaits of gold
With studs of silver.

THE SHULAMITE

While the king sat at his table,
My spikenard sent forth its fragrance.
My beloved is unto me as a bundle of myrrh,
That lieth betwixt my breasts.
My beloved is unto me as a cluster of henna-flowers
In the vineyards of En-gedi.

KING SOLOMON

Behold, thou art fair, my love; behold, thou art fair;
Thine eyes are as doves.

THE SHULAMITE

Behold, thou art fair, my beloved, yea, pleasant:
Also our couch is green.
The beams of our house are cedars,
And our rafters are firs.

I am a rose of Sharon,
A lily of the valleys.

KING SOLOMON

As a lily among thorns,
So is my love among the daughters.

THE SHULAMITE

As the apple tree among the trees of the wood,
So is my beloved among the sons.
I sat down under his shadow with great delight,
And his fruit was sweet to my taste.

He brought me to the banqueting house,
And his banner over me was love.
Stay ye me with raisins, comfort me with apples:
For I am sick of love.
His left hand is under my head,
And his right hand doth embrace me.
I adjure you, O daughters of Jerusalem,
By the roes, and by the hinds of the field,
That ye stir not up, nor awaken love,
Until it please.

Scene II

The voice of my beloved! behold, he cometh,
Leaping upon the mountains, skipping upon the hills.
My beloved is like a roe or a young hart:
Behold, he standeth behind our wall,
He looketh in at the windows,
He showeth himself through the lattice.
My beloved spoke, and said unto me,
"Rise up, my love, my fair one, and come away.
For, lo, the winter is past,
The rain is over and gone;
The flowers appear on the earth;
The time of the singing of birds is come,
And the voice of the turtle is heard in our land;
The fig tree ripeneth her green figs,
And the vines are in blossom,
They give forth their fragrance.
Arise, my love, my fair one, and come away.
O my dove, that art in the clefts of the rock, in the covert of
    the steep place,
Let me see thy countenance, let me hear thy voice;
For sweet is thy voice, and thy countenance is comely.

THE BROTHERS

Take us the foxes, the little foxes, that spoil the vineyards;
For our vineyards are in blossom.

THE SHULAMITE

My beloved is mine, and I am his:
He feedeth his flock among the lilies.

Until the day be cool, and the shadows flee away,
Turn, my beloved, and be thou like a roe or a young hart
Upon the mountains of Bether.
By night on my bed I sought him whom my soul loveth:
I sought him, but I found him not.
I said, "I will rise now, and go about the city,
In the streets and in the broad ways,
I will seek him whom my soul loveth":
I sought him, but I found him not.
The watchmen that go about the city found me:
To whom I said, "Saw ye him whom my soul loveth?"
It was but a little that I passed from them,
When I found him whom my soul loveth:
I held him, and would not let him go,
Until I had brought him into my mother's house,
And into the chamber of her that conceived me.

I adjure you, O daughters of Jerusalem,
By the roes, and by the hinds of the field,
That ye stir not up, nor awaken love,
Until it please.

Scene III

THE DAUGHTERS OF JERUSALEM

Who is this that cometh up out of the wilderness like pillars of
    smoke,
Perfumed with myrrh and frankincense,
With all powders of the merchant?

Behold, it is the litter of Solomon;
Threescore mighty men are about it,
Of the mighty men of Israel.

They all handle the sword, and are expert in war:
Every man hath his sword upon his thigh,
Because of fear in the night.

King Solomon made himself a palanquin
Of the wood of Lebanon.
He made the pillars thereof of silver,
The bottom thereof of gold, the seat of it of purple,
The midst thereof being paved with love,
From the daughters of Jerusalem.

Go forth, O ye daughters of Zion, and behold King Solomon,
With the crown wherewith his mother hath crowned him in the
    day of his espousals,
And in the day of the gladness of his heart.

KING SOLOMON

Behold, thou art fair, my love; behold, thou art fair;
Thine eyes are as doves behind thy veil:
Thy hair is as a flock of goats,
That lie along the side of Mount Gilead.
Thy teeth are like a flock of ewes that are newly shorn,
Which are come up from the washing;
Whereof every one hath twins,
And none is bereaved among them.

Thy lips are like a thread of scarlet,
And thy mouth is comely:
Thy temples are like a piece of a pomegranate
Behind thy veil.
Thy two breasts are like two fawns that are twins of a roe,
Which feed among the lilies.

Until the day be cool, and the shadows flee away,
I will get me to the mountain of myrrh,
And to the hill of frankincense.

Thou art all fair, my love;
And there is no spot in thee.
Come with me from Lebanon, my bride,
With me from Lebanon:
Look from the top of Amana,
From the top of Senir and Hermon,
From the lions' dens,
From the mountains of the leopards.
Thou hast ravished my heart, my sister, my bride;
Thou hast ravished my heart with one of thine eyes.
With one chain of thy neck.
How fair is thy love, my sister, my bride!
How much better is thy love than wine!
And the smell of thine ointments than all manner of spices!
Thy lips, O my bride, drop as the honeycomb:
Honey and milk are under thy tongue;
And the smell of thy garments is like the smell of Lebanon.

A garden shut up is my sister, my bride;
A spring shut up, a fountain sealed.
Thy shoots are an orchard of pomegranates, with precious fruits;
Henna with spikenard plants,
Spikenard and saffron,
Calamus and cinnamon, with all trees of frankincense;
Myrrh and aloes, with all the chief spices.
Thou art a fountain of gardens,
A well of living waters,
And flowing streams from Lebanon.

THE SHULAMITE

Awake, O north wind; and come, thou south;
Blow upon my garden, that the spices thereof may flow out.
Let my beloved come into his garden,
And eat his precious fruits.

KING SOLOMON

I am come into my garden, my sister, my bride:
I have gathered my myrrh with my spice;
I have eaten my honeycomb with my honey;
I have drunk my wine with my milk.
Eat, O friends;
Drink, yea, drink abundantly, O beloved.

Scene IV

THE SHULAMITE

I was asleep, but my heart waked:
It is the voice of my beloved that knocketh, saying,
"Open to me, my sister, my love, my dove, my undefiled:
For my head is filled with dew,
My locks with the drops of the night."
I have put off my coat; how shall I put it on?
I have washed my feet; how shall I defile them?
My beloved put in his hand by the hole of the door,
And my heart was moved for him.
I rose up to open to my beloved;
And my hands dropped with myrrh,
And my fingers with liquid myrrh,
Upon the handles of the bolt.

I opened to my beloved;
But my beloved had withdrawn himself, and was gone.
My soul had failed me when he spoke:
I sought him, but I could not find him;
I called him, but he gave me no answer.
The watchmen that go about the city found me,
They smote me, they wounded me;
The keepers of the walls took away my mantle from me.

I adjure you, O daughters of Jerusalem, if ye find my beloved,
That ye tell him, that I am sick of love.

THE DAUGHTERS OF JERUSALEM

What is thy beloved more than another beloved,
O thou fairest among women?
What is thy beloved more than another beloved,
That thou dost so adjure us?

THE SHULAMITE

My beloved is white and ruddy,
The chiefest among ten thousand.
His head is as the most fine gold,
His locks are bushy, and black as a raven.
His eyes are like doves beside the water brooks;
Washed with milk, and fitly set.
His cheeks are as a bed of spices, as banks of sweet herbs:

His lips are as lilies, dropping liquid myrrh.
His hands are as rings of gold set with beryl:
His body is as ivory work overlaid with sapphires.
His legs are as pillars of marble, set upon sockets of fine gold:
His aspect is like Lebanon, excellent as the cedars.

His mouth is most sweet: yea, he is altogether lovely.
This is my beloved, and this is my friend,
O daughters of Jerusalem.

THE DAUGHTERS OF JERUSALEM

Whither is thy beloved gone,
O thou fairest among women?
Whither hath thy beloved turned him,
That we may seek him with thee?

THE SHULAMITE

My beloved is gone to his garden, to the beds of spices,
To feed in the gardens, and to gather lilies.
I am my beloved's, and my beloved is mine:
He feedeth his flock among the lilies.

Scene V

KING SOLOMON

Thou art beautiful, O my love, as Tirzah,
Comely as Jerusalem,
Terrible as an army with banners.
Turn away thine eyes from me,
For they have overcome me.
Thy hair is as a flock of goats,
That lie along the side of Gilead.

Thy teeth are like a flock of ewes,
Which are come up from the washing;
Whereof every one hath twins,
And none is bereaved among them.

Thy temples are like a piece of pomegranate
Behind thy veil.

Who is she that looketh forth as the morning,
Fair as the moon,
Clear as the sun,
Terrible as an army with banners?

THE SHULAMITE

I went down into the garden of nuts,
To see the green plants of the valley,
To see whether the vine budded,
And the pomegranates were in flower.

THE DAUGHTERS OF JERUSALEM

Return, return, O Shulamite;
Return, return, that we may look upon thee.

KING SOLOMON

How beautiful are thy feet in sandals, O prince's daughter!
The joints of thy thighs are like jewels,
The work of the hands of a cunning workman.
Thy navel is like a round goblet,
Wherein no mingled wine is wanting:
Thy belly is like a heap of wheat
Set about with lilies.

Thy two breasts are like two fawns
That are twins of a roe.
Thy neck is like the tower of ivory;
Thine eyes as the pools in Heshbon, by the gate of Bathrabbim;

Thy nose is like the tower of Lebanon
Which looketh toward Damascus.

Thine head upon thee is like Carmel,
And the hair of thine head like purple;
The king is held captive in the tresses thereof.
How fair and how pleasant art thou,
O love, for delights!
This thy stature is like to a palm tree,
And thy breasts to clusters of grapes.
I said, "I will climb up into the palm tree,
I will take hold of the branches thereof":
Let thy breasts be as clusters of the vine,
And the smell of thy breath like apples;
And thy mouth like the best wine,
That goeth down smoothly for my beloved,
Gliding through the lips of those that are asleep.

THE SHULAMITE

I am my beloved's,
And his desire is toward me.
Come, my beloved, let us go forth into the field;
Let us lodge in the villages.
Let us get up early to the vineyards;
Let us see whether the vine hath budded, and its blossom be
    open,
And the pomegranates be in flower:

There will I give thee my love.
The mandrakes give forth fragrance,
And at our doors are all manner of precious fruits, new and
    old.
Which I have laid up for thee, O my beloved.

Oh that thou wert as my brother,
That sucked the breasts of my mother!
When I should find thee without, I would kiss thee;
Yea, and none would despise me.
I would lead thee, and bring thee into my mother's house
Who would instruct me;
I would cause thee to drink of spiced wine,
Of the juice of my pomegranate.
His left hand should be under my head,
And his right hand should embrace me.

I adjure you, O daughters of Jerusalem,
That ye stir not up, nor awaken love,
Until it please.

Scene VI

THE DAUGHTERS OF JERUSALEM

Who is this that cometh up from the wilderness,
Leaning upon her beloved?

KING SOLOMON

Under the apple tree I awakened thee:
There thy mother was in travail with thee,
There was she in travail that brought thee forth.

THE SHULAMITE

Set me as a seal upon thine heart, as a seal upon thine arm:
For love is strong as death;
Jealousy is cruel as the grave:
The flashes thereof are flashes of fire,

His mouth is most sweet: yea, he is altogether lovely.
This is my beloved, and this is my friend,
O daughters of Jerusalem.

THE DAUGHTERS OF JERUSALEM

Whither is thy beloved gone,
O thou fairest among women?
Whither hath thy beloved turned him,
That we may seek him with thee?

THE SHULAMITE

My beloved is gone to his garden, to the beds of spices,
To feed in the gardens, and to gather lilies.
I am my beloved's, and my beloved is mine:
He feedeth his flock among the lilies.

Scene V

KING SOLOMON

Thou art beautiful, O my love, as Tirzah,
Comely as Jerusalem,
Terrible as an army with banners.
Turn away thine eyes from me,
For they have overcome me.
Thy hair is as a flock of goats,
That lie along the side of Gilead.

Thy teeth are like a flock of ewes,
Which are come up from the washing;
Whereof every one hath twins,
And none is bereaved among them.

Thy temples are like a piece of pomegranate
Behind thy veil.

THE DAUGHTERS OF JERUSALEM

Who is she that looketh forth as the morning,
Fair as the moon,
Clear as the sun,
Terrible as an army with banners?

THE SHULAMITE

I went down into the garden of nuts,
To see the green plants of the valley,
To see whether the vine budded,
And the pomegranates were in flower.

THE DAUGHTERS OF JERUSALEM

Return, return, O Shulamite;
Return, return, that we may look upon thee.

KING SOLOMON

How beautiful are thy feet in sandals, O prince's daughter!
The joints of thy thighs are like jewels,
The work of the hands of a cunning workman.
Thy navel is like a round goblet,
Wherein no mingled wine is wanting:
Thy belly is like a heap of wheat
Set about with lilies.

Thy two breasts are like two fawns
That are twins of a roe.
Thy neck is like the tower of ivory;
Thine eyes as the pools in Heshbon, by the gate of Bathrabbim;

A very flame of the Lord.
Many waters cannot quench love,
Neither can the floods drown it:
If a man would give all the substance of his house for love
He would utterly be contemned.

THE BROTHERS

We have a little sister,
And she hath no breasts:
What shall we do for our sister
In the day when she shall be spoken for?
If she be a wall,
We will build upon her a turret of silver:
And if she be a door,
We will inclose her with boards of cedar.

THE SHULAMITE

I am a wall, and my breasts like the towers thereof:
Then was I in his eyes as one that found peace.
Solomon had a vineyard at Baal-hamon;
He let out the vineyard unto keepers;
Every one for the fruit thereof was to bring a thousand pieces
    of silver.
My vineyard, which is mine, is before me:
Thou, O Solomon, shalt have the thousand,
And those that keep the fruit thereof two hundred.

KING SOLOMON

Thou that dwellest in the gardens,
The companions hearken for thy voice:
Cause me to hear it.

Make haste, my beloved,
And be thou like to a roe or to a young hart
Upon the mountains of spices.

The Song of Solomon (King James Version)
set as a play by Ernest Sutherland Bates

My body, the horn,
The Boat of Heaven,
Is full of eagerness like the young moon.
My untilled land lies fallow.

Who will plow my body?
Who will plow my high field?
Who will plow my wet ground?

Who will station the ox there?
Who will plow my body?

Great Lady, the King will plow your body.
I the King will plow your body.

Then plow my body, man of my heart!
Plow my body! . . .

He has sprouted; he has burgeoned!
He is lettuce planted by the water.
He is the one my womb loves best . . .

My honey-man, my honey-man sweetens me always.
My lord, the honey-man of the gods . . .

Let the bed that rejoices the heart be prepared!
Let the bed that sweetens the loins be prepared!
Let the royal bed be prepared!

The bed is ready!
The bed is waiting!

The king went with lifted head to the holy loins.
He went to the queen with lifted head.
He opened wide his arms to the holy priestess of heaven.

from an ancient Sumerian sacred-wedding poem,
adapted from the translation by
Diane Wolkstein and Samuel Noah Kramer

As the mirror to my hand,
the flowers to my hair,
kohl to my eyes,
tambul to my mouth
musk to my breast
necklace to my throat,
ecstasy to my flesh,
heart to my home—

as wing to bird,
water to fish,
life to the living—
so you to me.

But tell me,
Madhava, beloved,
who are you?
Who are you really?

Vidyapati says, they are one another.

VIDYAPATI, Hindu love poem,
translation by Edward C. Dimock, Jr.,
and Denise Levertov

Let the earth of my body be mixed with the earth
my beloved walks on.
Let the fire of my body be the brightness
in the mirror that reflects his face.
Let the water of my body join the waters
of the lotus pool he bathes in.
Let the breath of my body be air
lapping his tired limbs.
Let me be sky, and moving through me
that cloud-dark Shyama, my beloved.

Hindu love poem,
translation by Edward C. Dimock, Jr.,
and Denise Levertov

. . . It is said by some that there is no fixed time or order
between the kiss and the pressing or scratching with the nails
or fingers, but that all these things should be done generally
before sexual union takes place, while striking and making the
various sounds generally takes place at the time of the union.
Vatsyayana, however, thinks that anything may take place at
any time, for love does not care for time or order. . . .

The following are the places for kissing, viz., the forehead, the eyes, the cheeks, the throat, the bosom, the breasts, the lips, and the interior of the mouth. Moreover the people of the Lat country kiss also the following places, viz., the joints of the thighs, the arms and the navel. But Vatsyayana thinks that though kissing is practiced by these people in the above places on account of the intensity of their love, and the customs of their country, it is not fit to be practiced by all.

Now in a case of a young girl there are three sorts of kisses, viz.:

> The nominal kiss.
> The throbbing kiss.
> The touching kiss.

1. When a girl only touches the mouth of her lover with her own, but does not herself do anything, it is called the "nominal kiss."

2. When a girl, setting aside her bashfulness a little, wishes to touch the lip that is pressed into her mouth, and with that object moves her lower lip, but not the upper one, it is called the "throbbing kiss."

3. When a girl touches her lover's lip with her tongue, and having shut her eyes, places her hands on those of her lover, it is called the "touching kiss."

Others authors describe four other kinds of kisses, viz.:

> The straight kiss.
> The bent kiss.
> The turned kiss.
> The pressed kiss.

1. When the lips of two lovers are brought into direct contact with each other, it is called a "straight kiss."

2. When the heads of two lovers are bent toward each other, and when so bent, kissing takes place, it is called a "bent kiss."

3. When one of them turns up the face of the other by holding the head and chin, and then kissing, it is called a "turned kiss."

4. Lastly, when the lower lip is pressed with much force, it is called a "pressed kiss."

There is also a fifth kind of kiss called the "greatly pressed kiss," which is effected by taking hold of the lower lip between two fingers, and then after touching it with the tongue, pressing it with great force with the lip.

When a man kisses the upper lip of a woman, while she in return kisses his lower lip, it is called the "kiss of the upper lip."

When one of them takes both the lips of the other between his or her own, it is called "a clasping kiss." A woman, however, only takes this kind of kiss from a man who has no moustache. And on the occasion of this kiss, if one of them touches the teeth, the tongue, and the palate of the other, with his or her tongue, it is called the "fighting of the tongue." In the same way, the pressing of the teeth of the one against the mouth of the other is to be practiced.

Kissing is of four kinds, viz., moderate, contracted, pressed, and soft, according to the different parts of the body which are kissed, for different kinds of kisses are appropriate for different parts of the body.

When a woman looks at the face of her lover while he is asleep, and kisses it to show her intention or desire, it is called a "kiss that kindles love."

When a woman kisses her lover while he is engaged in business, or while he is quarreling with her, or while he is looking at something else, so that his mind may be turned away, it is called a "kiss that turns away."

When a lover coming home late at night kisses his beloved who is asleep on her bed in order to show her his desire, it is called a "kiss that awakens." On such an occasion the woman may pretend to be asleep at the time of her lover's arrival, so that she may know his intention and obtain respect from him.

When a person kisses the reflection of the person he loves in a mirror, in water, or on a wall, it is called a "kiss showing the intention."

When a person kisses a child sitting on his lap, or a picture, or an image, or figure, in the presence of the person beloved by him, it is called a "transferred kiss."

When at night at a theatre, or in an assembly, a man coming up to a woman kisses a finger of her hand if she standing, or a toe of her foot if she be sitting, or when a woman in shampooing her lover's body, places her face in his thigh (as if she were sleepy) so as to inflame his passion, and kisses his thigh or great toe, it is called a "demonstrative kiss."

There is also a verse on this subject as follows:

"Whatever things may be done by one of the lovers to the other, the same should be returned by the other, i.e., if the woman kisses him he should kiss her in return; if she strikes him he should also strike her in return."

"On Kissing," from *The Kama Sutra of Vatsyayana:
The celebrated Hindu Treatise on Love*

Married men ought never to attempt or hurry their initial enterprise if they do not find themselves ready for it. If a man discovers himself to be agitated and on edge, it is better to give up outright any attempt at marital commerce and await a further occasion when he is less upset. . . . Women are to blame who receive us with that disdainful, squeamish and outraged air which, while it kindles us, snuffs us out. The daughter-in-law of Pythagoras rightly said that a woman who goes to bed with a man ought to take off her modesty along with her petticoat. . . .

Till possession be taken, our husband should leisurely and

by degrees make several little trials and light offers, without obstinately committing himself to an immediate conquest. Those who know their members to be naturally obedient need only guard themselves against an overwrought imagination.

We are right in remarking the untamed liberty of this member. He puffs himself up most importunately when we do not need him, and swoons away when our need is greatest. . . . Is there any member more rowdy and indiscreet?

When it comes to examples, I myself know one so rude and ungoverned that for forty years it has led its master in one continuous explosion, and is like to do so until he die of it. . . .

But let us proceed.

. . . A man, says Aristotle, must handle his wife with prudence, lest in tickling her too lasciviously, extreme pleasure makes her exceed the bounds of reason. What he says upon the account of conscience, physicians say for the sake of health: a pleasure excessively hot, voluptuous and frequent spoils the seed and hinders conceptions. . . . I for my part always went the plain way to work. . . .

Our poet, Virgil, describes a marriage blessed with concord and contentment and yet not over-loyal. . . . Let us confess the truth: there is hardly one of us who is not more afraid of being shamed by his wife's lapses than his own. . . . What an unjust scale of vices! . . . Lucullus, Caesar, Pompey, Antony, Cato and other good men were cuckolds and knew it, without making a fuss. In those days there was only one idiot, Lepidus, who died of grief from it. . . .

I see no marriages fail sooner than those based on beauty and amorous desires. More solid and durable foundations are necessary, and greater precautions. A boiling dashing ardor is worthless. Love and marriage are two goals approached by different and distinct paths. . . . Marriage has utility, justice, honor and constancy for its share. . . . Love builds itself wholly upon pleasure. . . . Marriage is a solemn and religious tie; and therefore the pleasure we take from it should be restrained, serious and seasoned with a certain gravity. . . . A good marriage—if there be any—rejects the company and conditions of love and seeks to reproduce those of friendship. It is a sweet companionship of life, full of trust and an infinite number of useful and solid services and mutual obligations. . . .

That few are observed to be happy is a token of its value and price. If well-formed and rightly taken, there is not a finer estate in human society. Though we cannot live without it, yet we do nothing but decry it. We see the same with bird-cages: the birds outside despair to get in and those within despair to get out.

Michel de Montaigne, from The Autobiography,
translation by Marvin Lowenthal

Abstinence sows sand all over
The ruddy limbs & flaming hair,
But Desire Gratified
Plants fruits of life & beauty there.

William Blake,
from The Notebook

"I have no name" . . .
What shall I call thee?
"I happy am,
Joy is my name."
Sweet joy befall thee!

Pretty joy! . . .
Sweet joy I call thee:

Thou dost smile,
I sing the while,
Sweet joy befall thee!

WILLIAM BLAKE,
from "Infant Joy"

When you came, you were like red wine and honey,
And the taste of you burnt my mouth with its sweetness.
Now you are like morning bread,
Smooth and pleasant.
I hardly taste you at all, for I know your savor;
But I am completely nourished.

AMY LOWELL, "A Decade"

I first tasted under Apollo's lips,
love and love sweetness,
I, Evadne;
my hair is made of crisp violets

or hyacinth which the wind combs back
across some rock shelf;
I, Evadne,
was made of the god of light.

His hair was crisp to my mouth,
as the flower of the crocus,
across my cheek,
cool as the silver-cress

on Erotos bank;
between my chin and throat,
his mouth slipped over and over.

Still between my arm and shoulder,
I feel the brush of his hair,
and my hands keep the gold they took,
as they wandered over and over,
that great arm-full of yellow flowers.

H.D., "Evadne"

Waking alone in a multitude of loves when morning's light
Surprised in the opening of her nightlong eyes
His golden yesterday asleep upon the iris
And this day's sun leapt up the sky out of her thighs
Was miraculous virginity old as loaves and fishes,
Though the moment of a miracle is unending lightning
And the shipyards of Galilee's footprints hide a navy of doves.

No longer will the vibrations of the sun desire on
Her deepsea pillow where once she married alone,
Her heart all ears and eyes, lips catching the avalanche
Of the golden ghost who ringed with his streams her mercury
    bone,
Who under the lids of her windows hoisted his golden luggage,
For a man sleeps where fire leapt down and she learns through
    his arm
That other sun, the jealous coursing of the unrivalled blood.

DYLAN THOMAS, "On the Marriage of a Virgin"

E. E. Cummings

there is a
moon sole
in the blue
night

    amorous of waters
tremulous,
blinded with silence the
undulous heaven yearns where

in tense starlessness
anoint with ardor
the yellow lover

stands in the dumb dark
svelte
and
urgent

    (again
love i slowly
gather
of thy languorous mouth the

thrilling
flower)

III

as is the sea marvelous
from god's

hands which sent her forth
to sleep upon the world

and the earth withers
the moon crumbles
one by one
stars flutter into dust

but the sea
does not change
and she goes forth out of hands and
she returns into hands

and is with sleep. . . .

love,
        the breaking

of your
            soul
            upon
my lips

                                from "Amores"

somewhere i have never travelled,gladly beyond
any experience,your eyes have their silence:
in your most frail gesture are things which enclose me,
or which i cannot touch because they are too near

your slightest look easily will unclose me
though i have closed myself as fingers,
you open always petal by petal myself as Spring opens
(touching skilfully, mysteriously)her first rose

or if your wish be to close me,i and
my life will shut very beautifully,suddenly,
as when the heart of this flower imagines
the snow carefully everywhere descending;

nothing which we are to perceive in this world equals
the power of your intense fragility:whose texture
compels me with the colour of its countries,
rendering death and forever with each breathing

(i do not know what it is about you that closes
and opens;only something in me understands
the voice of your eyes is deeper than all roses)
nobody,not even the rain, has such small hands

"somewhere i have never travelled"

. . . because two bodies, naked and entwined,
leap over time, they are invulnerable,
nothing can touch them, they return to the
        source,
there is no you, no I, no tomorrow,
no yesterday, no names, the truth of two
in a single body, a single soul,
oh total being . . .

OCTAVIO PAZ, from "Sunstone"

Now the great flower of the world
And its gold bee, the sun
With all its hives and lives of honeyed light . . .
Shall bless this youth and innocence—young people
Like the spring rainbows, risen from all growth,
The sap and singing, tall among the trees. . . .

The white bride and the forest of white flowers
Upon the Altar, and white lightnings of the dew
(Each drop Altair and Sirius) fallen from the petals
Seem one. And like the music of the air,
The young children following—
The bridesmaids with their curls as blond as water.

        Love is all life, the primal law,
The sun and planets to the husbandman,
The kernel and the sap; it is the power
That holds the Golden Rainers in the heavens, bringing us
The calyx of the flower of the world . . .
        Upon this happy day—
Even for the old, whose winter was flowerless, whose bones
    are sunless

(Yet older than Spring), their winter breaks again in flower
Till summer grows from a long-shadowed kiss . . .

. . . the lost floras of the world
Lie on young cheeks, young lips.

EDITH SITWELL, from "Prothalamium,"
written for the marriage of the Duke and Duchess of Kent, June 8, 1961

Denise Levertov

The ache of marriage:

thigh and tongue, beloved,
are heavy with it,
it throbs in the teeth

We look for communion
and are turned away, beloved,
each and each

It is leviathan and we
in its belly
looking for joy, some joy
not to be known outside it

two by two in the ark of
the ache of it.

"The Ache of Marriage"

My great brother
            Lord of the Song
wears the ruff of
            forest bear.

Husband, thy fleece of silk is black,
            a black adornment;
lies so close to the turns of the flesh,
burns my palm-stroke.

My great brother
            Lord of the Song

wears the ruff of
          forest bear . . .

Hair of man, man-hair, hair of
breast and groin, marking contour as
          silverpoint marks in cross-
          hatching, as river-
          grass on the woven current
          indicates ripple,
praise.

"A Psalm Praising
the Hair of Man's Body"

My black sun, my
Odessa sunflower,
spurs of Tartar gold
ring at your ankles,
you stand taller before me than the ten
towers of Jerusalem.

Your tongue has found
my tongue, peonies
turn their profusion towards
the lamp, it is you that burn there,
the Black Sea sings you awake.

Wake the violoncellos of Lebanon,
rub the bows with cedar resin,
wake the Tundra horsemen
to hunt tigers.
                    Your skin
tastes of the salt of Marmora,
the hair of your body casts
its net over me.

> To my closed eyes
> appears a curved
> horizon where darkness
> dazzles in your light. Your arms
> hold me from falling.

"Song for a Dark Voice"

expectation is our time
and waiting for you is best
so many evenings
flowered on the laughing sky

we are so alone
we hold hands
and even a cat is silent under a stove
and listens to how the rain falls

drops splash—those your feet
you are coming to me across gold puddles
your face is wet—I will kiss away the rain
come come

into my warm hands
into my waiting hands
into my greedy mouth
    like rain

HALINA POŚWIATOWSKA

There is nothing false in thee.
In thy heat the youngest body
Has warmth and light.
In thee the quills of the sun
Find adornment.
What does not die
Is with thee.

Thou art clothed in robes of music.
Thy voice awakens wings.

And still more with thee
Are the flowers of earth made bright.

Upon thy deeps the fiery sails
Of heaven glide.

Thou art the radiance and the joy.
Thy heart shall only fail
When all else has fallen.

What does not perish
Lives in thee.

KENNETH PATCHEN,
"There Is Nothing False in Thee"

I was wrapped in black
fur and white fur and
you undid me and then
you placed me in gold light
and then you crowned me,
while snow fell outside
the door in diagonal darts.

While a ten-inch snow
came down like stars
in small calcium fragments,
we were in our own bodies . . .
and you were in my body . . .
and at first I rubbed your
feet dry with a towel
because I was your slave
and then you called me princess.
Princess!

Oh then
I stood up in my gold skin
and I beat down the psalms
and I beat down the clothes
and you undid the bridle
and you undid the reins
and I undid the buttons,
the bones, the confusions,
the New England postcards,
the January ten o'clock night,

and we rose up like wheat,
acre after acre of gold,
and we harvested,
we harvested.

ANNE SEXTON, from "Us"

The wind blew all my wedding day,
And my wedding-night was the night of the high wind;
And a stable door was banging, again and again,
That he must go and shut it, leaving me

Stupid in the candlelight, hearing rain,
Seeing my face in the twisted candlestick,
Yet seeing nothing. When he came back
He said the horses were restless, and I was sad
That any man or beast that night should lack
The happiness I had.

Now in the day
All's ravelled under the sun by the wind's blowing.
He has gone to look at the floods, and I
Carry a chipped pail to the chicken-run,
Set it down, and stare. All is the wind
Hunting through clouds and forests, thrashing
My apron and the hanging cloths on the line.
Can it be borne, this bodying-forth by wind
Of joy my actions turn on, like a thread
Carrying beads? Shall I be let to sleep
Now this perpetual morning shares my bed?
Can even death dry up
These new delighted lakes, conclude
Our kneeling as cattle by all-generous waters?

PHILIP LARKIN, "Wedding Wind"

Lay your sleeping head, my love,
Human on my faithless arm;
. . . in my arms till break of day
Let the living creature lie,
Mortal, guilty, but to me,
The entirely beautiful.

Soul and body have no bounds:
To lovers as they lie upon

Her tolerant enchanted slope
In their ordinary swoon,
Grave the vision Venus sends
Of supernatural sympathy,
Universal love and hope . . .

W. H. AUDEN, from
"Lay Your Sleeping Head"

Body of my woman, I will live on through your
    marvelousness.
My thirst, my desire without end, my wavering road!
Dark river beds down which the eternal thirst is flowing,
and the fatigue is flowing, and the grief without shore.

PABLO NERUDA

I love it when you roll over and
lie on me in the dark, your weight
steady on me as tons of water, my
lungs like a little shut box, it
almost makes me faint to feel the
dry barbed surface of your legs
opening my legs, my heart swells like a
soft purple boxing glove and
then I love to lie there doing
nothing, my powerful arms thrown-down
bolts of muslin rippling at the selvage, your
pubic bone a pyramid laid
point-down on the point of another—
dazzling fulcrum! Then in the stillness and
night I love to feel you grow between my legs like a plant in fast motion, the

way in the auditorium in the
dark near the beginning of our lives we
sat by the hundreds and over our heads on the
bright screen the enormous flowers
unfolded in silence.

SHARON OLDS, "I Love It When"

O when the world's at peace
and every man is free
then will I go down unto my love.

O and I may go down
several times before that.

WENDELL BERRY,
"The Mad Farmer's Love Song"

You, because you love me, hold
Fast to me, caress me, be
Quiet and kind, comfort me
With stillness, say nothing at all.
You, because I love you, I
Am strong for you, I uphold
You. The water is alive
Around us. Living water
Runs in the cut earth between
Us. You, my bride, your voice speaks
Over the water to me.
Your hands, your solemn arms,
Cross the water and hold me.
Your body is beautiful.
It speaks across the water.
Bride, sweeter than honey, glad

Of heart, our hearts beat across
The bridge of our arms. Our speech
Is speech of the joy in the night
Of gladness. Our words live.
Our words are children dancing
Forth from us like stars on water.
My bride, my well beloved,
Sweeter than honey, than ripe fruit,
Solemn, grave, a flying bird,
Hold me. Be quiet and kind.
I love you. Be good to me.
I am strong for you. I uphold
You. The dawn of ten thousand
Dawns is afire in the sky.
The water flows in the earth.
The children laugh in the air.

KENNETH REXROTH,
"The Old Song and Dance"

VI

The Country of
Marriage

"She's my girl. . . . She's my blue sky. After sixteen years, I still bite her shoulders. She makes me feel like Hannibal crossing the Alps."

JOHN CHEEVER, from "The Country Husband"

When the vows are said, the ring or rings exchanged, and the symbolizing embrace shared, the now-married couple breaks out of the magic circle, turning their backs on the heavy baggage of ceremony. As they turn, they smile, and their happiness sheds light across the whole assembly of guests. For the couple, there now begins the time of adjustment and resolution, of learning one's capacity for shared labor in the new country, but quite as important for each individual, of exploring what poet Archibald MacLeish refers to as "the greatest and richest good—my own life to live."

I will reveal to you a love potion, without medicine, without herbs, without any witch's magic; if you want to be loved, then Love.

HECATON OF RHODES

There are three sights which warm my heart and are beautiful in the eyes of the Lord and of men: concord among brothers, friendship among neighbors, and a man and wife who are inseparable.

from The Wisdom of Ben Sira, Chapter 25, Verse 1

Come along! today is a festival!
Clap your hands and say, "This is a day of happiness!"
Who in the world is like this bridal pair?
The earth and the sky are full of sugar. Sugar cane is sprouting all around!
We can hear the roar of the pearly ocean. The whole world is full of waves!
The voices of Love are approaching from all sides. We are on our way to heaven!
Once upon a time we played with angels. Let's all go back up there again.

Heaven is our home! Yes, we are even higher up than heaven, higher than the angels!

My dear, it's true that spiritual beauty is wonderful. But your loveliness in this world is even more so!

JALAL AL-DIN RUMI, Persian love poem,
adapted from the translation by A. J. Arberry

> The moon shall be a darkness,
>   The stars give no light,
> If ever I prove false
>   To my heart's delight;
> In the middle of the ocean
>   Green grow the myrtle tree,
> If ever I prove false
>   To my Love that loves me.

ANONYMOUS

> My true love hath my heart and I have his,
>   By just exchange one for another given;
>   I hold his dear and mine he cannot miss;
>   There never was a better bargain driven:
>   My true love hath my heart and I have his.
>
> My heart in me keeps him and me in one;
>   My heart in him his thoughts and senses guides;
>   He loves my heart for once it was his own;
>   I cherish his because in me it bides:
>   My true love hath my heart and I have his.

SIR PHILIP SIDNEY, "My True Love Hath My Heart"

Sappho

Safe now. I've flown to you
like a child to its mother.

Is there in any land
any man whom you love
more than you love me?

I would go anywhere
to take you in my arms
again, my darling.

Translations by
Willis Barnstone

As the ant brought to Solomon the King
The thigh of a grass-hopper as an offering,
So do I bring my soul, beloved, to thee.

I have placed my head and my heart
On the sill of the door of my love.
Step gently, child!

Turkoman love song

My grief has ended. Comes now the season of joy.
For the flowers of Spring are jeweling my green garden.
Let us make ready to walk through its paths.
Go! Tell the nightingale that Spring is here.

And tell the minstrel to come with his lute.
Let him sing us a ballad of the flowers of Spring.
Do not listen to the parrot whispering to the rose
That Autumn will soon be here.

With spring my love returned to me,
And again I behold the moon of my delight.
Let others have their various festivals.
My only festival is when, in Spring,
I see my love's narrow feet
Step through the garden like lisping twin flowers.
Then Khushal Khan puts on his brightest robes
And enters the bazaar of his love's soft arms.

Afghan love song

My boat is of ebony,
the holes in my flute are golden.

As a plant takes out stains from silk
so wine takes sadness from the heart.

When one has good wine,
a graceful boat,
and a maiden's love,
why envy the immortal gods?

Li Tai Po, "Song on the River"

My boat glides swiftly
beneath the wide cloud-ridden sky,
and as I look into the river
I can see the clouds drift by the moon;
my boat seems floating
on the sky.

And thus I dream
my beloved is mirrored
on my heart.

Tu Fu, "On the River Tchou"

Take a lump of clay, wet it, pat it,
And make an image of me, and an image of you.
Then smash them, crash them, and add a little water.
Break them and remake them into an image of you
And an image of me.
Then in my clay, there's a little of you.
And in your clay, there's a little of me.
And nothing ever shall us sever;
Living, we'll sleep in the same quilt,
And dead, we'll be buried together.

Madame Kuan

'Tis the gift to be simple
'Tis the gift to be free
'Tis the gift to come down
Where we ought to be

And when we find ourselves
In the place just right
It will be in the valley
Of love and delight.

"Simple Gifts," a Shaker hymn

Love me little, love me long
Is the burden of my song;
Love that is too hot and strong, burneth all to waste;
Still I would not have thee cold,
Or backward or too bold,
For love that lasteth till 'tis old
Fadeth not in haste . . .

ANONYMOUS

Who shall have my fair lady!
Who but I, who but I, who but I?
Under the green leaves!
The fairest man
That best love can,
Under the green leaves!

ANONYMOUS

. . . Here upon earth, we'are Kings, and none but wee
Can be such Kings, nor of such subjects bee.
Who is so safe as wee? where none can doe

Treason to us, except one of us two.
    True and false feares let us refraine,
Let us love nobly, and live, and adde againe
Yeares and yeares unto yeares, till we attaine
To write threescore . . .

JOHN DONNE, from "The Anniversarie"

I wonder by my troth, what thou, and I
Did, till we lov'd? were we not wean'd till then?
But suck'd on countrey pleasures, childishly?
Or snorted we in the seaven sleepers den?
T'was so; But this, all pleasures fancies bee.
If ever any beauty I did see,
Which I desir'd, and got, t'was but a dreame of thee.

And now good morrow to our waking soules,
Which watch not one another out of feare;
For love, all love of other sights controules,
And makes one little roome, an every where.
Let sea-discoverers to new worlds have gone,
Let Maps to other, worlds on worlds have showne,
Let us possesse one world, each hath one, and is one.

My face in thine eye, thine in mine appeares,
And true plaine hearts doe in the faces rest,
Where can we finde two better hemispheares
Without sharpe North, without declining West?
What ever dyes, was not mixt equally;
If our two loves be one, or, thou and I
Love so alike, that none doe slacken, none can die.

JOHN DONNE, "The Good-Morrow"

Marriage is a sweet state,
I can affirm it by my own experience,
In very truth, I who have a good and wise husband
Whom God helped me to find.
I give thanks to him who will save him for me,
For I can truly feel his great goodness
And for sure the sweet man loves me well.

Throughout that first night in our home,
I could well feel his great goodness,
For he did me no excess
That could hurt me.
But, before it was time to get up,
He kissed me 100 times, this I affirm,
Without exacting further outrage,
And yet for sure the sweet man loves me well.

He used to say to me in his soft language:
"God brought you to me,
Sweet lover, and I think he raised me
To be of use to you."
And then he did not cease to dream
All night, his conduct was so perfect,
Without seeking other excesses.
And yet for sure the sweet man loves me well.

O Princes, yet he drives me mad
When he tells me he is all mine;
He will destroy me with his gentle ways,
And yet for sure the sweet man loves me well.

CHRISTINE DE PISAN, "In Praise of Marriage,"
translation by C. Meredith Jones

A wreathed garland of deserved praise,
Of praise deserved, unto thee I give,
I give to thee, who knowest all my wayes,
My crooked winding wayes, wherein I live,
Wherein I die, not live: for life is straight,
Straight as a line, and ever tends to thee,
To thee, who art more farre above deceit,
Then deceit seems above simplicitie.
Give me simplicitie that I may live,
So live and like, that I may know thy wayes,
Know them and practise them: then shall I give
For this poore wreath, give thee a crown of praise.

GEORGE HERBERT, "A Wreath"

She is gentle and also wise;
Of all other she beareth the prize,
    That ever I saw.

To hear her sing, to see her dance!
She will the best herself advance,
    That ever I saw.

To see her fingers that be so small!
In my conceit she passeth all
    That ever I saw.

Nature in her hath wonderly wrought.
Christ, never such another bought
    That ever I saw.

I have seen many that have beauty
Yet is there none like to my lady
    That ever I saw.

Therefore I dare boldly say,
I shall have the best and fairest may
That ever I saw.

Anonymous

My love to my husband was not only a matrimonial love, as betwixt man and wife, but a natural love, as the love of brethren, parents, and children, also a sympathetical love, as the love of friends, likewise a customary love, as the love of acquaintances, a loyal love, as the love of a subject, an obedient love, as the love to virtue, an uniting love, as the love of soul and body, a pious love, as the love to heaven, all which several loves did meet and intermix, making one mass of love.

Anonymous

If ever two were one, then surely we.
If ever man were lov'd by wife, then thee;
If ever wife was happy in a man,
Compare with me ye women if you can.
I prize thy love more than whole Mines of gold,
Or all the riches that the East doth hold.
My love is such that Rivers cannot quench,
Nor ought but love from thee, give recompence.
Thy love is such I can no way repay,
The heavens reward thee manifold I pray.
Then while we live, in love let's so persever,
That when we live no more, we may live ever.

Anne Bradstreet, "To my Dear and loving Husband"

Come live with me and be my love,
And we will all the pleasures prove
That hills and valleys, dales and fields
And all the craggy mountains yields.

There we will sit upon the rocks
And see the shepherds feed their flocks,
By shallow rivers to whose falls
Melodious birds sing madrigals.

And I will make thee beds of roses
With a thousand fragrant posies,
A cap of flowers and a kirtle
Embroidered all with leaves of myrtle.

A gown made of the finest wool
Which from our pretty lambs we pull;
Fair lined slippers for the cold,
With buckles of the purest gold;

A belt of straw and ivy buds,
With coral clasps and amber studs:
And if these pleasures may thee move,
Come live with me and be my love.

The shepherds' swains shall dance and sing
For thy delight each May morning:
If these delights thy mind may move,
Then live with me and be my love.

CHRISTOPHER MARLOWE,
"The Passionate Shepherd to His Love"

I did not live until this time
　　Crown'd my felicity,
When I could say without a crime,
　　I am not thine, but thee.

This carcass breath'd, and walkt, and slept,
　　So that the world believ'd
There was a soul the motions kept;
　　But they were all deceiv'd.

For as a watch by art is wound
　　To motion, such was mine:
But never had Orinda found
　　A soul till she found thine;

Which now inspires, cures and supplies,
　　And guides my darkned breast:
For thou art all that I can prize,
　　My joy, my life, my rest. . . .

KATHERINE PHILIPS, from
"To My Excellent Lucasia, on Our Friendship"

O my heart's heart, and you who are to me
　　More than myself myself, God be with you,
　　Keep you in strong obedience leal and true
To Him whose noble service setteth free;
Give you all good we see or can foresee,
　　Make your joys many and your sorrows few,
　　Bless you in what you bear and what you do,
Yea, perfect you as He would have you be. . . .

CHRISTINA ROSSETTI, from
"Monna Innominata: A Sonnet of Sonnets"

. . . Your hands lie open in the long fresh grass,
The finger-points look through like rosy blooms:
Your eyes smile peace. The pasture gleams and glooms
'Neath billowing skies that scatter and amass.
All round our nest, far as the eye can pass,
Are golden kingcup-fields with silver edge
Where the cow-parsley skirts the hawthorn-hedge.
'Tis visible silence, still as the hour-glass.
Deep in the sun-searched growths the dragon-fly
Hangs like a blue thread loosened from the sky:—
So this winged hour is dropped to us from above.
Oh! clasp we to our hearts, for deathless dower,
This close-companioned inarticulate hour
When twofold silence was the song of love. . . .

DANTE GABRIEL ROSSETTI, from "The House of Life"

. . . The mairie was a mile and a half from the farm, and they
went thither on foot, returning in the same way after the ceremony in the church. The procession, first united like one long
coloured scarf that undulated across the fields, along the narrow
path winding amid the green corn, soon lengthened out, and
broke up into different groups that loitered to talk. The fiddler
walked in front with his violin, gay with ribbons at its pegs.
Then came the married pair, the relations, the friends, all following pell-mell; the children stayed behind amusing themselves plucking the bellflowers from oat-ears, or playing
amongst themselves unseen. Emma's dress, too long, trailed a
little on the ground; delicately, with her gloved hands, she
picked off the coarse grass and the thistledowns. . . .
    The table was laid under the cart-shed. On it were four
sirloins, six chicken fricassées, stewed veal, three legs of mutton,

and in the middle a fine roast sucking-pig, flanked by four chitterlings with sorrel. At the corners were decanters of brandy. Sweet bottled-cider frothed round the corks, and all the glasses had been filled to the brim with wine beforehand. Large dishes of yellow cream, that trembled with the least shake of the table, had designed on their smooth surface the initials of the newly wedded pair in nonpareil arabesques. A confectioner of Yvetot had been intrusted with the tarts and sweets. As he had only just set up in the place, he had taken a lot of trouble, and at dessert he himself brought in a set dish that evoked loud cries of wonderment. To begin with, at its base there was a square of blue cardboard, representing a temple with porticoes, colonnades, and stucco statuettes all round, and in the niches constellations of gilt paper stars; then on the second stage was a dungeon of Savoy cake, surrounded by many fortifications in candied angelica, almonds, raisins and quarters of oranges; and finally, on the upper platform a green field with rocks set in lakes of jam, nutshell boats, and a small Cupid balancing himself in a chocolate swing whose two uprights ended in real roses for balls at the top.

Until night they ate. When any of them were too tired of sitting, they went out for a stroll in the yard, or for a game with corks in the granary, and then returned to table. Some towards the finish went to sleep and snored. But with the coffee every one woke up. Then they began songs, showed off tricks, raised heavy weights, performed feats with their fingers, then tried lifting carts on their shoulders, made broad jokes, kissed the women. At night when they left, the horses, stuffed up to the nostrils with oats, could hardly be got into the shafts; they kicked, reared, the harness broke, their masters laughed or swore; and all night in the light of the moon along country roads there were runaway carts at full gallop plunging into the ditches, jumping over yard after yard of stones, clambering up the hills, with women leaning out from the tilt to catch hold of the reins.

Those who stayed at the Bertaux spent the night drinking in the kitchen. The children had fallen asleep under the seats.

The bride had begged her father to be spared the usual marriage pleasantries. However, a fishmonger, one of their cousins (who had even brought a pair of soles for his wedding present), began to squirt water from his mouth through the keyhole, when old Rouault came up just in time to stop him, and explain to him that the distinguished position of his son-in-law would not allow of such liberties. . . .

Gustave Flaubert, from *Madame Bovary*,
translation by Eleanor Marx

SONNET XIV

If thou must love me, let it be for nought
Except for love's sake only. Do not say,
"I love her for her smile—her look—her way
Of speaking gently,—for a trick of thought
That falls in well with mine, and certes brought
A sense of pleasant ease on such a day"—
For these things in themselves, Beloved, may
Be changed, or change for thee,—and love, so wrought,
May be unwrought so. Neither love me for
Thine own dear pity's wiping my cheeks dry,—
A creature might forget to weep, who bore
Thy comfort long, and lose thy love thereby!
But love me for love's sake, that evermore
Thou mayest love on, through love's eternity.

Elizabeth Barrett Browning, from *Sonnets from the Portuguese*

How do I love thee? Let me count the ways.
I love thee to the depth and breadth and height
My soul can reach, when feeling out of sight
For the ends of Being and ideal Grace.
I love thee to the level of everyday's
Most quiet need, by sun and candle-light.
I love thee freely, as men strive for Right;
I love thee purely, as they turn from Praise.
I love thee with the passion put to use
In my old griefs, and with my childhood's faith.
I love thee with a love I seemed to lose
With my lost saints,—I love thee with the breath,
Smiles, tears, of all my life!—and, if God choose,
I shall but love thee better after death.

ELIZABETH BARRETT BROWNING, from *Sonnets from the Portuguese*

What greater thing is there for two human souls than to feel that they are joined . . . to strengthen each other . . . to be at one with each other in silent unspeakable memories.

GEORGE ELIOT

Marriage is terrifying, but so is a cold and forlorn old age. . . . marriage, if comfortable, is not at all heroic. It certainly narrows and damps the spirits of generous men. In marriage, a man becomes slack and selfish and undergoes a fatty degeneration of his moral being . . . the air of the fireside withers out all the fine wildings of the husband's heart. He is so comfortable and happy that he begins to prefer comfort and happiness to everything else on earth, his wife included. . . . Twenty years ago, this man was equally capable of crime or heroism; now he is fit for neither. His soul is asleep, and you may speak without constraint; you will not wake him. . . . For women there is less of this danger. Marriage is of so much use to a woman, opens out to her so much more of life, and puts her in the way of so much more freedom and usefulness, that, whether she marry ill or well, she can hardly miss some benefit. It is true, however, that some of the merriest and most genuine of woman are old maids. . . .

A certain sort of talent is almost indispensable for people who would spend years together and not bore themselves to death. . . . to dwell happily together, they should be versed in the niceties of the heart, and born with a faculty for willing compromise . . . should laugh over the same sort of jests and have many . . . an old joke between them which time cannot wither nor custom stale. . . . You could read Kant by yourself if you wanted, but you must share a joke with someone else. You can forgive people who do not follow you through a philosophical disquisition; but to find your wife laughing when you had tears in your eyes, or staring when you were in a fit of laughter, would go some way towards a dissolution of the marriage. . . . Certainly, if I could help it, I would never marry a wife who wrote.

[For a woman] a ship captain is a good man to marry . . . for absences are a good influence in love. . . . It is to be noticed that those who have loved once or twice already are so much the better educated to a woman's hand. . . . Lastly, no woman should marry a teetotaller, or a man who does not smoke. . . .

A man expects an angel for a wife; [yet] he knows that she is like himelf—erring, thoughtless and untrue; but like himself also, filled with a struggling radiancy of better things. . . . You may safely go to school with hope; but ere you marry, should have learned the mingled lesson of the world: that hope and love address themselves to a perfection never realised, and yet, firmly held, become the salt and staff of life; that you yourself are compacted of infirmities . . . and yet you have a something in you lovable and worth preserving; and that, while the mass of mankind lies under this scurvy condemnation, you will scarce find one but, by some generous reading, will become to you a lesson, a model and a noble spouse through life. So thinking, you will constantly support your own unworthiness and easily forgive the failings of your friend. Nay, you will be wisely glad that you retain the . . . blemishes; for the faults of married people continually spur up each of them, hour by hour, to do better and to meet and love upon a higher ground.

Robert Louis Stevenson, from *Virginibus Puerisque*

When you are old and gray and full of sleep,
And nodding by the fire, take down this book,
And slowly read, and dream of the soft look
Your eyes had once, and of their shadows deep;

How many loved your moments of glad grace,
And loved your beauty with love false or true;
But one man loved the pilgrim soul in you,
And loved the sorrows of your changing face . . .

William Butler Yeats,
from "When You Are Old"

I propose to speak . . . of a troth that is observed *by virtue of the absurd*—that is to say, simply because it has been pledged— and by virtue of being an absolute which will uphold husband and wife as persons. Fidelity, it must be admitted, stands emphatically athwart the stream of values nowadays admired by nearly every one. Fidelity is extremely *unconventional*. It contradicts the general belief in the revelatory value of both spontaneity and manifold experiences. It denies that in order to remain lovable a beloved must display the greatest possible *number* of qualities. It denies that its own goal is happiness. It offensively asserts first, that its aim is obedience to a Truth that is believed in, and secondly, that it is the expression of a wish to be constructive. For fidelity is not in the least a sort of conservatism, but rather a construction. An "absurdity" quite as much as passion, it is to be distinguished from passion by its persistent refusal to submit to its own dream, by its persistent need of acting in behalf of the beloved, by its being persistently in contact with a reality which it seeks to control, not to flee.

I maintain that fidelity thus understood sets up the person. For the person is manifested like something made, in the widest sense of making. It is built up as a thing is made, thanks to a making, and in the same conditions as we make things, its first condition being a fidelity to something that before was not, but now is in process of being created. Person, made thing, fidelity— the three terms are neither separable nor separately intelligible. All three presuppose that a stand has been taken, and that we have adopted what is fundamentally the attitude of creators. Hence in the humblest lives the plighting of a troth introduces the opportunity of making and of rising to the plane of the person—on condition, of course, that the pledge has not been for "reasons" in the giving of which there is a reservation which will allow those reasons to be repudiated some day when they have ceased to appear "reasonable"! The pledge exchanged in marriage is the very type of a *serious* act, because it is a pledge given once and for all. The irrevocable alone is serious. Every life, even the most disinherited one, has some immediate potentiality of dignity, and it is in an 'absurd' fidelity that this dignity may be attained—in a readiness to say "No" to a dazzling passion, when there is every earthly reason for saying "Yes." . . .

In marriage the loving husband or wife vows fidelity first of all to *the other* at the same time as to his or her true self . . . the fidelity of the married couple is acceptance of one's fellow-creature, a willingness to take the other as he or she is in his or her intimate particularity. Let me insist that fidelity in marriage cannot be merely that negative attitude so frequently imagined; it must be active. To be content not to deceive one's wife or husband would be an indication of indigence, not one of love. Fidelity demands far more: it wants the good of the beloved, and when it acts in behalf of that good it is creating in its own presence the neighbour. And it is by this roundabout way through the other that the self rises into being a person— beyond its own happiness. Thus as persons a married couple are a mutual creation, and to become persons is the double achievement of "active love." What denies both the individual and his natural egotism is what constructs a person. At this point faithfulness in marriage is discovered to be the law of a new life. . . .

DENIS DE ROUGEMONT, from Love in the Western World

The essence of a good marriage is respect for each other's personality combined with that deep intimacy, physical, mental, and spiritual, which makes a serious love between man and woman the most fructifying of all human experiences. Such love, like everything that is great and precious, demands its own morality, and frequently entails a sacrifice of the less to the greater; but such sacrifice must be voluntary, for, where it is not, it will destroy the very basis of the love for the sake of which it is made.

BERTRAND RUSSELL, from Marriage and Morals

. . . man, like woman, is flesh, therefore passive, the plaything of his hormones and of the species, the restless prey of his desires. And she, like him, in the midst of the carnal fever, is a consenting, a voluntary gift, an activity; they live out in their several fashions the strange ambiguity of existence made body. In those combats where they think they confront one another, it is really against the self that each one struggles, projecting into the partner that part of the self which is repudiated; instead of living out the ambiguities of their situation, each tries to make the other bear the abjection and tries to reserve the honor for the self. If, however, both should assume the ambiguity with a clear-sighted modesty, correlative of an authentic pride, they would see each other as equals and would live out their erotic drama in amity. The fact that we are human beings is infinitely more important than all the peculiarities that distinguish human beings from one another. . . .

It is nonsense to assert that revelry, vice, ecstasy, passion, would become impossible if man and woman were equal in concrete matters; the contradictions that put the flesh in opposition to the spirit, the instant to time, the swoon of immanence to the challenge of transcendence, the absolute of pleasure to the nothingness of forgetting, will never be resolved; in sexuality will always be materialized the tension, the anguish, the joy, the frustration, and the triumph of existence. To emancipate woman is to refuse to confine her to the relations she bears to man, not to deny them to her; let her have her independent existence and she will continue none the less to exist for him *also*: mutually recognizing each other as subject, each will yet remain for the other an *other*. The reciprocity of their relations will not do away with the miracles—desire, possession, love, dream, adventure—worked by the division of human beings into two separate categories; and the words that move us—giving, conquering, uniting—will not lose their meaning. On the contrary, when we abolish the slavery of half of humanity, together with the whole system of hyprocrisy that it implies, then the 'division' of humanity will reveal its genuine significance and the human couple will find its true form.

Simone de Beauvoir, from *The Second Sex*,
translation by H. M. Parshley

No wandering any more where the feet stumble
Upon a sudden rise, or sink in damp
Marsh grasses. No uncertain following on
With nothing there to follow—a sure bird,
A fence, a farmhouse. No adventuring now
Where motion that is yet not motion dies.
Circles have lost their magic, and the voice
Comes back upon itself. . . . The road is firm.
It runs, and the dust is not too deep, and the end
Never can heave in sight—though one is there.
It runs in a straight silence, till a word
Turns it; then a sentence, and evening falls
At an expected inn, whose barest room
Cannot be lonely if a hand is reached
To touch another hand, the walls forgotten. . . .
Laughter is morning, and the road resumes;
Adventurous, it never will return.

Mark Van Doren, "Marriage"

Slowly, slowly wisdom gathers:
Golden dust in the afternoon,
Somewhere between the sun and me,
Sometimes so near that I can see,
Yet never settling, late or soon.

Would that it did, and a rug of gold
Spread west of me a mile or more:
Not large, but so that I might lie
Face up, between the earth and sky,
And know what none has known before.

Then I would tell as best I could
The secrets of that shining place:
The web of the world, how thick, how thin,
How firm, with all things folded in;
How ancient, and how full of grace.

MARK VAN DOREN, "Slowly, Slowly Wisdom Gathers"

Like everything which is not the involuntary result of fleeting
emotion, but the creation of time and will, any marriage, happy
or unhappy, is infinitely more interesting and significant than
any romance, however passionate.

W. H. AUDEN

When women as well as men emerge from biological living to
realize their human selves, [their later] halves of life may become
their years of greatest fulfillment. . . . when women do not need
to live through their husbands and children, men will not fear
the love and strength of women, nor need another's weakness
to prove their own masculinity. They can finally see each other

as they are. And this may be the next step in human evolution.

Who knows what women can be when they are finally free to become themselves? Who knows what women's intelligence will contribute when it can be nourished without denying love? Who knows of the possibilities of love when men and women share not only children, home, and garden, not only the fulfillment of their biological roles, but the responsibilities and passions of the work that creates the human future and the full human knowledge of who they are? It has barely begun, the search of women for themselves. But the time is at hand. . . .

BETTY FRIEDAN, from *The Feminine Mystique*

Here are a man and a woman, being married.
The entire world of summer lawns
holds its breath for the event. The trees
around them are lovely, displaying the small
breath and motions of August. The couple glance
at one another. Where has the moon gone,
the requisite moon? Nearby, a mother
begs her child, "Try to remember;
when did you have it last?" Oh,
impossible mystery. Where is joy
when it is not here? Time says nothing.
These things can happen, and will,
while children at the yard's border play
among grown-ups tasting the summer's wine.

Memory looks at its watch, smiling.
The moon will begin to come round
the way it always did but we'd forgotten.

The lovers touch hands and think of
some place they want to be, and go there.
The child, happy at last,
has remembered where its lost ball is.
In the garden the pink phlox and the lilies
show off, between the old moon
here in the hot sky and the one to come.
Everyone hugs or shakes hands
and walks off toward the future, waving.
The man and woman look at each other.
They know it means happiness, this year. They do.

DAVID KELLER, from "Afternoon,
in a Back Yard on Chestnut Street"

The truth has never been of any real value to any human being.
It is a symbol for mathematicians and philosophers to pursue.
In human relations, kindness and lies are worth a thousand
truths.

GRAHAM GREENE, from *The Heart of the Matter*

Though you know it anyhow
Listen to me, darling, now,

Proving what I need not prove
How I know I love you, love.

Near and far, near and far,
I am happy where you are;

Likewise I have never learnt
How to be it where you aren't.

Far and wide, far and wide,
I can walk with you beside;

Furthermore, I tell you what,
I sit and sulk where you are not.

Visitors remark my frown
When you're upstairs and I am down,

Yes, and I'm afraid I pout
When I'm indoors and you are out;

But how contentedly I view
Any room containing you.

In fact I care not where you be,
Just as long as it's with me.

In all your absences I glimpse
Fire and flood and trolls and imps.

Is your train a minute slothful?
I goad the stationmaster wrothful.

When with friends to bridge you drive
I never know if you're alive,

And when you linger late in shops
I long to telephone the cops.

Yet how worth the waiting for,
To see you coming through the door.

Somehow, I can be complacent
Never but with you adjacent.

Near and far, near and far,
I am happy where you are;

Likewise, I have never learnt
How to be it where you aren't.

Then grudge me not my fond endeavor,
To hold you in my sight forever;

Let none, not even you, disparage
Such valid reason for a marriage.

OGDEN NASH, "Tin Wedding Whistle"

—Muses, whose worship I may never leave
but for this pensive woman, now I dare,
teach me her praise! with her my praise receive.—

Three years already of the round world's war
had rolled by stoned & disappointed eyes
when she and I came where we were made for.

Pale as a star lost in returning skies,
more beautiful than midnight stars more frail
she moved towards me like chords, a sacrifice;

entombed in body trembling through the veil
arm upon arm, learning our ancient wound,
we see our one soul heal, recovering pale.

Then priestly sanction, then the drop of sound.
Quickly part to the cavern ever warm
deep from the march, body to body bound,

descend (my soul) out of dismantling storm
into the darkness where the world is made.
Come back to the bright air. Love is multiform.

Heartmating hesitating unafraid
although incredulous, she seemed to fill
the lilac shadow with light wherein she played,

whom sorry childhood had made sit quite still,
an orphan silence, unregarded sheen,
listening for any small soft note, not hopeful:

caricature: as once a maiden Queen,
flowering power comeliness kindness grace,
shattered her mirror, wept, would not be seen.

These pities moved. Also above her face
serious or flushed, swayed her fire-gold
not earthly hair, now moonless to unlace,

resistless flame, now in a sun more cold
great shells to whorl about each secret ear,
mysterious histories, strange shores, unfold.

New musics! One the music that we hear
this is the music which the masters make
out of their minds, profound solemn & clear.

And then the other music, in whose sake
all men perceive a gladness but we are drawn
less for that joy than utterly to take

our trial, naked in the music's vision,
the flowing ceremony of trouble and light,
all Loves becoming, none to rest upon.

Such Mozart made,—an ear so delicate
he fainted at a trumpet-call, a child
so delicate. So merciful that sight,

so stern, we follow rapt who ran awild.
Marriage is the second music, and thereof
we hear what we can bear, faithful & mild. . . .

JOHN BERRYMAN, from "Canto Amor"

March 22: On Sunday evening with the children in bed and
Pauline writing letters I talked to K [the author's husband]:
". . . I'm learning to milk the cow. I'm going to take over your
afternoon's work sometimes and you can have the time for
more study. I can chop wood and feed the fowls. We'll share
the time."

"I can't possibly allow you to do rough work, chop wood
and do the fowls. Not when you have the desire and the ability
and the opportunity to do what you do."

I was surprised to hear this.

He continued, " . . . People who can do the work you do
should be allowed to do it and those who can't should hew the
wood and draw the water, feed the fowls, chop and wood and
milk Susie."

This distressed me.

He went on, "There's no need for you to take on my afternoon work."

"But my work loses its value unless you are happy. Everything loses its value. Your contentment comes before my work."

"I'm happy."

"No you're not."

He looked at me with interest. I went on, "You're not getting
as much time for study as I am. You're the real mother of this
family; I'm just one of the children. We must share the time."

He pushed the kettle over the flames. "But your study means more to you than mine does to me."

"I question it. But in any case that's not my point. Your work means more to me than my own does to me because your work involves your contentment and that comes before my work with me."

He was interested but looked doubtful.

"It's the truth," I added. "Unless you are happy in your work mine is valueless to me."

K examined my face as though he was seeing it for the first time.

"It may not be apparent," I said, "but I love you and you come first in the world with me, before everything, before anybody. You and the children. My family and home are more to me than my work. If it came to the choice it would be my work that went overboard. No doubt I've appeared to be a failure in the home but that is not indicative. Do you feel I've failed you in the home?" I called on all my courage to ask this question which could draw a devastating answer.

He put out two cups and saucers. "Well, it has crossed my mind that you shouldn't have married."

Catastrophe! "But I've been a good mother! Look at me all through my babies. How I stuck to them . . ."

"Yes. But, what I mean is that a person, any person, with your inclinations should not marry. You should have gone on with your work. Marriage has sidetracked you."

Desperately on the defensive, "I wash and dress the little boys in the morning, and Jonquil. I feed them."

"I know. What I mean is that people like you with talents and ideas should be undisturbed by marriage."

"Ah . . . but you see! I wouldn't have had these desires at all if I hadn't married. When I didn't teach and had no babies I hardly lifted a brush. Hardly did a thing. The *need* to study, to do, to make, to think, *arises* from being married. I need to be married to work."

He poured the boiling water on the tea. "I still think that you should be allowed your work in preference to my being allowed mine. Your desire is stronger than mine."

"That's quite possible. But I'm still going to hurry up and learn to milk Susie."

We had tea, ran off the dishes and went to bed. Neither of us lowered the flag, neither won, and we haven't talked about that since, but the part about his coming before my work must have registered and held for there's been a tenderness in his manner toward me like the reappearance of the sun. . . .

November 12: Hurrying up the road in the rain I reflected on my position in my small vital circle and my influence on them:
. . . When I'm unhappy my sorrow and violence cast all about me and everybody pays, right down to the baby, whereas now with my impulses back in their normal channel, now that I am happy . . . our home—at least my home—is incredibly joyful.

I am aware of how much I mean to each one. . . . For some reason that is obscure to me they all turn to me and seek my love and I pour on them *thousands* of kisses. . . . My mouth, my face, my waist, my breasts, my hands . . . sheer common property. . . . I'm the one without whose goodnight kiss no one will go to bed. At this time I'm first with them all. Why does each need my love so much? You'd think my elusiveness in continual slipping away would lessen their call on me. . . .

How long will this last? I wonder. It was not always like this in the past . . . so shy in my adolescence, so apart in my childhood . . . and cannot always be. Some day I may be looking back on these days when arms were endlessly round my neck, my body seldom my own; some day I may find myself sitting at a table with all the silence I want, possibly more than I want. There may be large echoing rooms and corridors, and stairs and stunning views, none of which would put its arms round my neck and want to make love to me, call to me in the night. . . .

Now that I feel better, temporarily, I must honor all this love by trying to be gentler and kinder, by forgiving more readily and teaching more sensitively. Love has the quality of informing almost everything—even one's work.

Sylvia Ashton-Warner, from Myself

You learned from me that commitment, love, loyalty, "being there" are at the center of everything. I taught you, by example, that life is very complex, that there are no final solutions, there is only the commitment to the search for quality and genuineness. I taught you to treasure the real and to shun the plastic. I taught you to value human relationships, to run away from bigotry and to expose it when you find it. I taught you to believe in the value of books, to respect education and learning, to admire goodness and integrity and wisdom. Let's not forget humor. Above all, perhaps, I taught you by example that a thoughtful and examined life requires difficult choices; that there are, for such a life, no instant fixes. We live in a society which sells trivial answers for every complex human dilemma. In our household, from our example, you were able to draw on a different set of strengths, not available in the ambient society of your growing up. I see all of these strengths in your life now. You have become the kind of woman I dreamed of raising.

Renée Haenel Levine, letter to her daughter

The darkness lifts, imagine, in your lifetime.
There you are—cased in clean bark you drift
through weaving rushes, fields flooded with cotton.

You are free. The river films with lilies,
shrubs appear, shoots thicken into palm. And now
all fear gives way: the light
looks after you, you feel the waves' goodwill
as arms widen over the water; Love,

the key is turned. Extend yourself—
it is the Nile, the sun is shining,
everywhere you turn is luck.

                    LOUISE GLÜCK, "The Undertaking"

I knew a woman, lovely in her bones,
When small birds sighed, she would sigh back at them;
Ah, when she moved, she moved more ways than one:
The shapes a bright container can contain!
Of her choice virtues only gods should speak,
Or English poets who grew up on Greek
(I'd have them sing in chorus, cheek to cheek).

How well her wishes went! She stroked my chin,
She taught me Turn, and Counter-turn, and Stand;
She taught me Touch, that undulant white skin;
I nibbled meekly from her proffered hand;
She was the sickle; I, poor I, the rake,
Coming behind her for her pretty sake
(But what prodigious mowing we did make).

Love likes a gander, and adores a goose:
Her full lips pursed, the errant note to seize;
She played it quick, she played it light and loose;
My eyes, they dazzled at her flowing knees;
Her several parts could keep a pure repose,
Or one hip quiver with a mobile nose
(She moved in circles, and those circles moved).

Let seed be grass, and grass turn into hay:
I'm martyr to a motion not my own;
What's freedom for? To know eternity.
I swear she cast a shadow white as stone.
But who would count eternity in days?
These old bones live to learn her wanton ways:
(I measure time by how a body sways).

THEODORE ROETHKE, "I Knew a Woman"

My lizard, my lively writher,
May your limbs never wither,
May the eyes in your face
Survive the green ice
Of envy's mean gaze;
May you live out your life
Without hate, without grief,
And your hair ever blaze,
In the sun, in the sun,
When I am undone,
When I am no one.

THEODORE ROETHKE,
"Wish for a Young Wife"

Beautiful, my delight,
Pass, as we pass the wave.
Pass, as the mottled night
Leaves what it cannot save,
Scattering dark and bright.

Beautiful, pass and be
Less than the guiltless shade
To which our vows were said;

Less than the sound of the oar
To which our vows were made,—
Less than the sound of its blade
Dipping the stream once more.

LOUISE BOGAN, "To be Sung on the Water"

All has been translated into treasure:
Weightless as amber,
Translucent as the currant on the branch,
Dark as the rose's thorn.

Where is the shimmer of evil?
This is the shell's iridescence
And the wild bird's wing.

Ignorant, I took up my burden in the wilderness.
Wise with great wisdom, I shall lay it down upon flowers.

LOUISE BOGAN, from "After the Persian"

This institution,
perhaps one should say enterprise
out of respect for which
one says one need not change one's mind
about a thing one has believed in,
requiring public promises

of one's intention
to fulfil a private obligation:
I wonder what Adam and Eve
think of it by this time,
this fire-gilt steel
alive with goldenness;
how bright it shows— . . .

Below the incandescent stars
below the incandescent fruit,
the strange experience of beauty;
its existence is too much . . .

"Everything to do with love is mystery;
it is more than a day's work
to investigate this science."
One sees that it is rare—
that striking grasp of opposites
opposed each to the other, not to unity,
which in cycloid inclusiveness
has dwarfed the demonstration
of Columbus with the egg— . . .

MARIANNE MOORE, from "Marriage"

This poem is for my wife
I have made it plainly and honestly
The mark is on it
Like the burl on the knife

I have not made it for praise
She has no more need for praise
Than summer has
On the bright days

In all that becomes a woman
Her words and her ways are beautiful
Love's lovely duty
The well-swept room

Wherever she is there is sun
And time and a sweet air
Peace is there
Work done

There are always curtains and flowers
And candles and baked bread
And a cloth spread
And a clean house

Her voice when she sings is a voice
At dawn by a freshening sea
Where the wave leaps in the
Wind and rejoices

Wherever she is it is now
It is here where the apples are
Here in the stars
In the quick hour

The greatest and richest good—
My own life to live—
This she has given me

If giver could

       ARCHIBALD MACLEISH, "Poem in Prose"

Samuel Menashe

You whose name I know
As well as my own
You whose name I know
But not to tell
You whose name I know
Yet do not say
Even to myself—
You whose name I know
Know that I came
Here to name you
Whose name I know

"Whose Name I Know"

O Many Named Beloved
Listen to my praise
Various as the seasons
Different as the days
All my treasons cease
When I see your face

"Many Named"

A-
round
my neck
an amu-
let
Be-
tween

my eyes
a star
A
ring
in my
nose
and a
gold
chain
to
Keep me
where
You
are

"A-"

Having come unto
the tall house of our habit
where it settles rump downward
on its stone foundations
in the manner of a homely brood mare
who throws good colts

and having entered
where sunlight is pasted on the windows
ozone rises from the mullions
dust motes pollinate the hallway
and spiders remembering a golden age
sit one in each drain

we will hang up our clothes and our vegetables
we will decorate the rafters with mushrooms
on our hearth we will burn splits of silver popple
we will stand up to our knees in their flicker
the soup kettle will clang five notes of pleasure
and love will take up quarters.

MAXINE KUMIN, "Homecoming"

We have come in the winter
To this warm country room,
The family and friends
Of the bride and the groom,
To bring them our blessing,
To share in their joy,
And to hope that years passing
The best measures employ
 To protect their small clearing,
 And their love be enduring.

May the hawk that flies over
These thick-wooded hills,
Where through tangled ground cover
With its cushion of quills
The plump porcupine ambles
And the deer come to browse
While through birches and brambles
Clear cold water flows,
 Protect their small clearing,
 And their love be enduring.

May the green leaves returning
To rock maples in spring
Catch fire, and, still burning,
Their flaming coat fling
On the lovers when sleeping
To contain the first chill
Of crisp autumn weather
With log-fires that will
Protect their small clearing,
And their love be enduring.

May the air that grows colder
Where the glacier has left
Its erratic boulder
Mountain water has cleft,
And the snow then descending
No less clear than their love
Be a white quilt depending
From sheer whiteness above
To protect their small clearing,
And their love be enduring.

WILLIAM JAY SMITH,
"Song for a Country Wedding"
For Deborah and Marc

I believe that living is an act of creativity and that, at certain moments in our lives, our creative imaginations are more conspicuously demanded than at others. At certain moments, the need to decide upon the story of our own lives becomes particularly pressing—when we choose a mate, for example . . .

... every marriage [is] a narrative construct—or two narrative constructs. In unhappy marriages, I see two versions of reality rather than two people in conflict. I see a struggle for imaginative dominance going on. Happy marriages seem to me those in which the two partners agree on the scenario they are enacting. . . . marriage seems to me a subjectivist fiction with two points of view often deeply in conflict, sometimes fortuituously congruent.

Marriages go bad not when love fades—love can modulate into affection without driving two people apart—but when this understanding about the balance of power breaks down. . . .

PHYLLIS ROSE, from *Parallel Lives: Five Victorian Marriages*

Funny the way the healing comes
in a northeaster, rain sliding
sideways across the glass, the waves
beaching themselves, rolling home
across the gray water, running before the wind
boxing the spruce and cedars fat with resistance.

Russian olives and beach plum,
stripped to their bird-bone branches
blackened with rain against the still
green lawn, jerk and twitch, stiff
with cold; offering so little
to the blow, they bend, barely.

Even from the bay window, clouds
are near, putting a ceiling on the sky
trying to slip off the water through a slit

of dove-gray on the horizon. Only
gulls are nervy enough to fly
in this weather. They, too, slide

sideways, behind the rain, wings
spread wide, grabbing the currents
and sledding across the wind, as if
they were made for a northeaster, designed
all gray with flashes of white
to match its color. Banking,

they turn into the wind and wobble,
their backsides to us, heading away, small,
unsteady as a child learning to walk
the hard way. Inside, all the things God gives
that were always there, all that's man-made
keeping us, the light bulbs glowing

through yellowed parchment shades
shedding seventeenth-century light, filling in
the shadow of our daughter, the fire
toasting the room, Gershwin and Porter
coming from Public Radio in a braid
of complicated notes, a music written

before we were born, surviving in a changed
world, and this good man holding me, I
holding him, as we glide in Top-Siders
across the rug, seeing each other return
sliding sideways into our eyes
this side of the glass.

MARY STEWART HAMMOND,
"Slow Dancing in the Living Room: Thanksgiving"

Wendell Berry

How hard it is for me, who live
in the excitement of women
and have the desire for them
in my mouth like salt. Yet
you have taken me and quieted me.
You have been such light to me
that other women have been
your shadows. You come near me
with the nearness of sleep.
And yet I am not quiet.
It is to be broken. It is to be
torn open. It is not to be
reached and come to rest in
ever. I turn against you,
I break from you, I turn to you.
We hurt, and are hurt,
and have each other for healing.
It is healing. It is never whole.

"Marriage"

One faith is bondage. Two
are free. In the trust
of old love, cultivation shows
a dark graceful wilderness
at its heart. Wild
in that wilderness, we roam
the distances of our faith,
safe beyond the bounds

of what we know. O love,
open. Show me
my country. Take me home.

"A Homecoming"

1.

I dream of you walking at night along the streams
of the country of my birth, warm blooms and the nightsongs
of birds opening around you as you walk.
You are holding in your body the dark seed of my sleep.

2.

This comes after silence. Was it something I said
that bound me to you, some mere promise
or, worse, the fear of loneliness and death?
A man lost in the woods in the dark, I stood
still and said nothing. And then there rose in me,
like the earth's empowering brew rising
in root and branch, the words of a dream of you
I did not know I had dreamed. I was a wanderer
who feels the solace of his native land
under his feet again and moving in his blood.
I went on, blind and faithful. Where I stepped
my track was there to steady me. It was no abyss
that lay before me, but only the level ground.

3.

Sometimes our life reminds me
of a forest in which there is a graceful clearing
and in that opening a house,
an orchard and garden,
comfortable shades, and flowers
red and yellow in the sun, a pattern

made in the light for the light to return to.
The forest is mostly dark, its ways
to be made anew day after day, the dark
richer than the light and more blessed,
provided we stay brave
enough to keep on going in.

4.

How many times have I come to you out of my head
with joy, if ever a man was,
for to approach you I have given up the light
and all directions. I come to you
lost, wholly trusting as a man who goes
into the forest unarmed. It is as though I descend
slowly earthward out of the air. I rest in peace
in you, when I arrive at last.

5.

. . . You are the known way leading always to the unknown,
and you are the known place to which the unknown is always
leading me back. More blessed in you than I know,
I possess nothing worthy to give you, nothing
not belittled by my saying that I possess it.
Even an hour of love is a moral predicament, a blessing
a man may be hard up to be worthy of. He can only
accept it, as a plant accepts from all the bounty of the light
enough to live, and then accepts the dark,
passing unencumbered back to the earth, as I
have fallen time and again from the great strength
of my desire, helpless, into your arms.

6.

What I am learning to give you is my death
to set you free of me, and me from myself
into the dark and the new light. Like the water

of a deep stream, love is always too much. We
did not make it. Though we drink till we burst
we cannot have it all, or want it all.
In its abundance it survives our thirst.
In the evening we come down to the shore
to drink our fill, and sleep, while it
flows through the regions of the dark.
It does not hold us, except we keep returning
to its rich waters thirsty. We enter,
willing to die, into the commonwealth of its joy.

7.
I give you what is unbounded, passing from dark to dark,
containing darkness: a night of rain, an early morning.
I give you the life I have let live for love of you:
a clump of orange-blooming weeds beside the road,
the young orchard waiting in the snow, our own life
that we have planted in this ground, as I
have planted mine in you. I give you my love for all
beautiful and honest women that you gather to yourself
again and again, and satisfy—and this poem,
no more mine than any man's who has loved a woman.

from "The Country of Marriage"

VII

Morning in Eternal Space

Here I must say, a little anyhow: what I can hardly hope to bear out in the record: that a house of simple people which stands empty and silent in the vast Southern country morning sunlight, and everything which on this morning in eternal space it by chance contains . . . shines quietly forth such grandeur, such sorrowful holiness of its exactitudes in existence: as no human consciousness shall ever rightly perceive . . . : that there can be more beauty and more deep wonder in the standings and spacings of mute furnishings on a bare floor between the squaring bourns of walls than in any music ever made: that this square home, as it stands in unshadowed earth between the winding years of heaven, is, not to me but of itself, one among the serene and final, uncapturable beauties of existence: that this beauty is made between hurt but invincible nature and the plainest cruelties and needs of human existence in this uncured time, and is inextricable among these and as impossible without them as a saint born in paradise.

JAMES AGEE, from *Let Us Now Praise Famous Men*

The wedding ceremony per se *is over. For a few moments, the couple may wish to gather their thoughts in privacy: Jewish tradition makes a point of that need, specifying a short retreat for the two alone before the festivities begin. Then the guests and wedding party gather to exchange toasts to the new family, to beloved forebears and absent friends and relatives.*

In many parts of the world, however, the wedding cycle carries on with libations to the earth—gifts of corn, rice, oil, wine, spilled on the ground as invitation to the spirits to join the party. These joyous but serious rituals of integration of the newly married couple into the cycles of nature shed their power over projected time to come, even to the time, long in the future, of inevitable separation and loss. Thoughts of that order are not inappropriate to a wedding. The house of which James Agee speaks, which we call the house of marriage, stands under "the winding years of heaven" and is both lived in and vacated according to their measure. But it stands in ring upon ring of fields, hills, horizon, sky, and stars, whose embrace never falters, in which the love passed down human generations seems to our questing minds even to live on in the mode we call eternity.

The following prayers and blessings from many lands and ages lift the curtain, as I said before, on that vast landscape which can be for a courageous couple their true country. It may seem strange to find invocations to and praises of the sun, wind, thunder, and other natural powers in a book on weddings. But we are born out of and return to their order of being, and our state of "marriage" in the largest sense must be to them.

So . . . libations to all gods!

Libations, then dancing!

And then to sleep, in a place only the Wintu Indian knows.

The Fountains mingle with the River
    And the Rivers with the Ocean,
The winds of Heaven mix for ever
    With a sweet emotion;
Nothing in the world is single;
    All things by a law divine
In one spirit meet and mingle.
    Why not I with thine?—

See the mountains kiss high Heaven
    And the waves clasp one another;
No sister-flower would be forgiven
    If it disdained its brother,
And the sunlight clasps the earth
    And the moonbeams kiss the sea:
What is all this sweet work worth
    If thou kiss not me?

PERCY BYSSHE SHELLEY, "Love's Philosophy"

. . . Therefore, on every morrow, are we wreathing
A flowery band to bind us to the earth.
Spite of despondence, of the inhuman dearth
Of noble natures, of the gloomy days,
Of all the unhealthy and o'erdarkened ways

Made for our searching: yes, in spite of all,
Some shape of beauty moves away the pall
From our dark spirits . . .

John Keats, from "Endymion"

Live you by love confined,
There is no nearer nearness;
Break not his light bounds,
The stars' and seas' harness:
There is nothing beyond,
We have found the land's end.
We'll take no mortal wound
Who felt him in the furnace,
Drowned in his fierceness,
By his midsummer browned:
Nor ever lose awareness
Of nearness and farness
Who've stood at earth's heart careless
Of suns and storms around,
Who have leant on the hedge of the wind,
On the last ledge of darkness . . .

C. Day Lewis, from "Live You by Love"

When the white fog burns off,
the abyss of everlasting light
is revealed. The last cobwebs
of fog in the
black firtrees are flakes
of white ash in the world's hearth.

Cold of the sea is counterpart
to this great fire. Plunging
out of the burning cold of ocean
we enter an ocean of intense
noon. Sacred salt
sparkles on our bodies.

After mist has wrapped us again
in fine wool, may the taste of salt
recall to us the great depths about us.

Denise Levertov, "The Depths"

Now that I have your face by heart, I look
Less at its features than its darkening frame
Where quince and melon, yellow as young flame,
Lie with quilled dahlias and the shepherd's crook.
Beyond, a garden. There, in insolent ease
The lead and marble figures watch the show
Of yet another summer loathe to go
Although the scythes hang in the apple trees.

Now that I have your face by heart, I look.

Now that I have your voice by heart, I read
In the black chords upon a dulling page
Music that is not meant for music's cage,
Whose emblems mix with words that shake and bleed.
The staves are shuttled over with a stark
Unprinted silence. In a double dream
I must spell out the storm, the running stream.
The beat's too swift. The notes shift in the dark.

Now that I have your voice by heart, I read.

Now that I have your heart by heart, I see
The wharves with their great ships and architraves;
The rigging and the cargo and the slaves
On a strange beach under a broken sky.
O not departure, but a voyage done!
The bales stand on the stone; the anchor weeps
Its red rust downward, and the long vine creeps
Beside the salt herb, in the lengthening sun.

Now that I have your heart by heart, I see.

LOUISE BOGAN, "Song for the Last Act"

I will woo her, I will go with her into the wilderness and comfort her: there I will restore her vineyards, turning the Vale of Trouble into the Gate of Hope, and there she will answer as in her youth, when she came up out of Egypt. On that day she shall call me, "My husband . . ."

Then I will make a covenant on behalf of Israel with the wild beasts, the birds of the air, and the things that creep on the earth, and I will break bow and sword and weapon of war and sweep them off the earth, so that all living creatures may lie down without fear. I will betroth you to myself forever, betroth you in lawful wedlock with unfailing devotion and love; I will betroth you to myself to have and to hold, . . . I will answer for the heavens, and they will answer for the earth, and the earth will answer for the corn, the new wine and the oil.

Hosea 2:14–15; 18–23 (New English Bible)

I invoke thee, who art the greatest of all, who created all, who generated it from thyself, who sees all and is never seen. Thou hast given to the sun its glory and its power, to the moon hast thou granted the right to wax and wane and follow a regular course, without having robbed anything from other regions, but having been equal with all. For at thy appearance the world came into being and there was light. All things bowed down before thee, whom no one can contemplate in thy true form, who changes form, who remains the invisible Ayion of the Ayion.

Greek prayer to the god Ayion

O Morning Star! when you look down upon us, give us peace and refreshing sleep. Great Spirit! bless our children, friends, and visitors through a happy life. May our trails lie straight and level before us. Let us live to be old. We are all your children and ask these things with good hearts.

Hymn of the Great Plains Indians to the sun

O Spirit, grant us a calm lake, little wind, little rain, so that the canoes may proceed well, so that they may proceed speedily.

Tanganyikan fishermen's prayer

May you be for us a moon of joy and happiness. Let the young become strong and the grown man maintain his strength, the pregnant woman be delivered and the woman who has given birth, suckle her child. Let the stranger come to the end of his journey and those who remain at home dwell safely in their houses. Let the flocks that go to feed in the pastures return happily. May you be a moon of harvest and of calves. May you be a moon of restoration and of good health.

African prayer to the new moon

The year is abundant, with much millet and rice;
And we have our high granaries,
With myriads, and hundreds of thousands, and millions of
    measures in them
For spirits and sweet spirits,
To present to our ancestors, male and female,
And to supply all our ceremonies.
The blessings sent down on us are of every kind.

Chinese prayer of thanksgiving

I humbly ask that this Palace, as far downward as the lowermost
rock-roots, suffer no harm from reptiles among its bottom-
ropes; as far upward as the blue clouds are diffused in the Plain
of High Heaven, suffer no harm from flying birds in the celestial
smoke-hole; that the joinings of the firmly planted pillars, and
of the crossbeams, rafters, doors, and windows may not move
or make a noise, that there may be no slackening of the tied
rope-knots and no dishevelment of the roof-thatch, no creaking
of the floor-joints or alarms by night.

I humbly ask that the gods guard the great eight road-forks
like a mighty assemblage of rocks. . . .

Whenever, from the Root-country, the Bottom-country, there
come savage and unfriendly beings, consort not and parley not
with them; but if they go below, keep watch below; if they go
above, keep watch above, protecting us against pollution with
a night guarding and with a day guarding. The offerings I
furnish in your honor are bright cloth, shining cloth, soft cloth,
and rough cloth. Of *sake* I fill the bellies of the jars. Grain I
offer you. Of things that dwell in the mountains and on the
moors I offer the soft of hair and the coarse of hair. Of things

that dwell in the blue sea-plain, the broad of fin and the narrow
of fin, even to the weeds of the shallows and the weeds of the
shore.

Japanese invocation to the spirits to protect the Palace

Fly ahead of me.
Open the way,
Prepare the path.
O spirit of the sun
That dwells in the jungle-south,
O mother of light
Who are jealous.
I turn to thee, imploring
Keep your shadows high, very high!
And you who dwell in the west on the mountaintop,
O my lordly forebear of the great strength,
The powerful hill.
Come to me!
And you, venerable charmer of the flames,
With the gray beard.
I implore thee!
Give approval to all my thoughts
And to all my desires.
Listen to me,
Listen to all my prayers, all my prayers!

. . .

All together let us smoke tobacco,
Let us all drink wine.
All together let us ride a horse.

Let us all wear furs.
We shall not keep hidden
What we have learned.
We shall preserve
What we have found.

. . .

We have decided here and now to marry our son and daughter.
Therefore, O goddess of Fire, hearken and be witness. Protect
this pair from every illness; watch over them so that they may
grow old.

Three Turko-Mongolian prayers

You are my [husband/wife]
My feet shall run because of you.
My feet, dance because of you.
My heart shall beat because of you.
My eyes, see because of you.
My mind, think because of you.
And I shall love because of you.

Eskimo love song

O, You who dwell in Tsegihi,
In the house made of dawn,
In the house made of evening twilight,
In the house made of dark cloud,
In the house made of the he-rain, of the dark mist,
In the house made of the she-rain, of pollen, of grasshoppers,
Where the dark mist curtains the doorway,
The path to which is the rainbow,

Where the zigzag lightning stands high on top,
Oh, divinity!
With your moccasins of dark cloud, come to us,
With your leggings and shirt and headdress of dark cloud, come
    to us,
With your head enveloped in dark cloud, come to us,
With the dark thunder above you, come to us, soaring,
With the shapen cloud at your feet, come to us, soaring,
With the far darkness made of the dark cloud over your head,
    come to us, soaring.
With the far darkness made of the rain and the mist over your
    head, come to us, soaring.
With the zigzag lightning flung out on high over your head,
With the rainbow hanging high over your head, come to us,
    soaring.
With the far darkness made of the dark cloud on the ends of
    your wings,
With the far darkness made of the rain and the mist on the ends
    of your wings, come to us, soaring.
With the zigzag lightning, with the rainbow hanging high on
    the ends of your wings, come to us, soaring.
With the near darkness made of the dark cloud of the he-rain
    and the she-rain, come to us,
With the darkness on the earth, come to us.
With these I wish the foam floating on the flowing water over
    the roots of the great corn.
I have made your sacrifice,
I have prepared a smoke for you,
My feet restore for me.
My limbs restore, my body restore, my mind restore, my voice
    restore for me.
Today, take out your spell for me,
Today, take away your spell for me,

Away from me you have taken it,
Far off from me it is taken,
Far off you have done it.
Happily I recover,
Happily I become cool,
My eyes regain their power, my head cools, my limbs regain
    the strength, I hear again.
Happily I walk; impervious to pain, I walk; light within, I walk;
    joyous, I walk.
Abundant dark clouds I desire,
An abundance of vegetation I desire,
An abundance of pollen, abundant dew, I desire.
Happily may fair white corn, to the ends of the earth, come
    with you.
Happily may fair yellow corn, fair blue corn, fair corn of all
    kinds, plants of all kinds, goods of all kinds, jewels of all
    kinds, to the ends of the earth, come with you.
With these before you, happily may they come with you,
With these behind, below, above, around you, happily may
    they come with you,
Thus you accomplish your tasks.
Happily, the old men will regard you,
Happily, the old women will regard you,
The young men and the young women will regard you,
The children will regard you,
The chiefs will regard you,
Happily, as they scatter in all directions, they will regard you.
Happily, as they approach their homes, they will regard you.
May their roads home be on the trail of peace,
Happily may they all get back.
In beauty I walk,
With beauty before me, I walk,
With beauty behind me, I walk,

With beauty below and above me, in the beauty about me, I
    walk.
It is finished in beauty.
It is finished in beauty.
It is finished in beauty.

Navajo hymn to the Thunderbird,
translation by Washington Matthews

To the West:

Over there are the mountains. May you see them as long as
you live, for from them you receive sweet pine for incense.

To the North:

Strength will come from the North. May you look for many
years upon the Star that never moves.

To the East:

Old age will come from below, from where comes the light
of the Sun.

To the South:

May warm winds of the South bring you food.

Blackfoot prayer to the four directions

To the Mound of the East: Spring

Under the influence of the vernal yang, the vegetation is reborn.
The time of fertilizing rains, the time of love.

The thunder sounds and wakes the hibernating creatures.
That which seemed dead revives, and pursues its destiny.

May the innumerable new beings live their life to its end.
May the crowd of the living fully enjoy the happiness of the
    vernal spring.

To the Mound of the South: Summer

The red light grows, heat increases,
The flowering trees are in full splendor.

After the flowers will come fruits, plentiful and savory . . .

To the Mound of the West: Autumn

The West is the region of white light.
Autumn wind gently kills the vegetation.
But the seeds of the plants are preserved.
They contain the germ of the spring to come.

To the Mound of the North: Winter

Somber is the region of the North. All beings which hibernate
    have gone into the earth.
Vegetables have lose their leaves, and frost freezes the land . . .
May the people, remembering their origin, retain love for
    simplicity. . . .
May they make offerings, may they prepare the lands, in order
    that their next harvest may be abundant.

Chinese prayer to the four directions

Ten thousand things bright
Ten thousand miles, no dust
Water and sky one color
Houses shining along your road.

Chinese blessing

The life in us is like the water in the river. It may rise this year higher than man has ever known it, and flood the parched uplands; even this may be the eventful year, which will drown out all our muskrats. It was not always dry land where we dwell. I see far inland the banks which the stream anciently washed, before science began to record its freshets. Every one has heard the story which has gone the rounds of New England, of a strong and beautiful bug which came out of the dry leaf of an old table of apple-tree wood, which had stood in a farmer's kitchen for sixty years, first in Connecticut, and afterward in Massachusetts,—from an egg deposited in the living tree many years earlier still, as appeared by counting the annual layers beyond it; which was heard gnawing out for several weeks, hatched perchance by the heat of an urn. . . . Who knows what beautiful and winged life, whose egg has been buried for ages under many concentric layers of woodenness in the dead dry life of society, deposited at first in the alburnum of the green and living tree, which has been gradually converted into the semblance of its well-seasoned tomb,—heard perchance gnawing out now for years by the astonished family of man, as they sat round the festive board,—may unexpectedly come forth from amidst society's most trivial and handselled furniture, to enjoy its perfect summer life at last!

. . . such is the character of that morrow which mere lapse of time can never make to dawn. The light which puts out our eyes is darkness to us. Only that day dawns to which we are awake. There is more day to dawn. The sun is but a morning star.

HENRY DAVID THOREAU, from Walden

How enduring are our bodies, after all! The forms of our brothers and sisters, our parents and children and wives, lie still in the hills and fields around us.

HENRY DAVID THOREAU, from *The Journal*

To the dim light and the large circle of shade
I have clomb, and to the whitening of the hills,
There where we see no color in the grass.
Natheless my longing loses not its green,
It has so taken root in the hard stone
Which talks and hears as though it were a lady.

Utterly frozen is this youthful lady,
Even as the snow that lies within the shade;
For she is no more moved than is the stone
By the sweet season which makes warm the hills
And alters them afresh from white to green
Covering their sides again with flowers and grass.

When on her hair she sets a crown of grass
The thought has no more room for other lady,
Because she weaves the yellow with the green
So well that Love sits down there in the shade,—
Love who has shut me in among low hills
Faster than between walls of granite-stone.

She is more bright than is a precious stone;
The wound she gives may not be healed with grass:
I therefore have fled far o'er plains and hills
For refuge from so dangerous a lady;
But from her sunshine nothing can give shade,—
Not any hill, nor wall, nor summer-green.

A while ago, I saw her dressed in green,—
So fair, she might have wakened in a stone
This love which I do feel even for her shade;
And therefore, as one woos a graceful lady,
I wooed her in a field that was all grass
Girdled about with very lofty hills.

Yet shall the streams turn back and climb the hills
Before Love's flame in this damp wood and green
Burn, as it burns within a youthful lady,
For my sake, who would sleep away in stone
My life, or feed like beasts upon the grass,
Only to see her garments cast a shade.

How dark soe'er the hills throw out their shade,
Under her summer-green the beautiful lady
Covers it, like a stone cover'd in grass.

> CINO DA PISTOIA, "Sestina of the Lady Pietra
> degli Scrovigni," translation by Dante Gabriel Rossetti

I found her out there
On a slope few see,
That falls westwardly
To the salt-edged air,
Where the ocean breaks
On the purple strand,
And the hurricane shakes
The solid land.

I brought her here,
And have laid her to rest
In a noiseless nest
No sea beats near.

She will never be stirred
In her loamy cell
By the waves long heard
And loved so well.

So she does not sleep
By those haunted heights
The Atlantic smites
And the blind gales sweep,
Whence she often would gaze
At Dundagel's famed head,
While the dipping blaze
Dyed her face fire-red;

And would sigh at the tale
Of sunk Lyonnesse,
As a wind-tugged tress
Flapped her cheek like a flail;
Or listen at whiles
With a thought-bound brow
To the murmuring miles
She is far from now.

Yet her shade, maybe,
Will creep underground
Till it catch the sound
Of that western sea
As it swells and sobs
Where she once domiciled,
And joy in its throbs
With the heart of a child.

THOMAS HARDY,
"I Found Her Out There"

I want to paint men and women with that something of the
eternal which the halo used to symbolize . . . to express the
love of two lovers by a wedding of two complementary colors,
their mingling and opposition, the mysterious vibration of
kindred tones. To express the thought of a brow by the radiance
of a light tone against a somber background.

   To express hope by some star, the eagerness of a soul by a
sunset radiance.

Vincent van Gogh, from a letter to his brother, Theo

This we know, all things are connected, like the blood which
unites one family. All things are connected. Whatever befalls
the earth, befalls the sons of the earth. Man did not weave the
web of life; he is merely a strand in it. Whatever he does to
the web, he does to himself.

Chief Seattle of the Dwamish Tribe

Blessed is the light that turns to fire, and blessed the
    flames that fire makes of what it burns.
Blessed the inexhaustible sun, for it feeds the moon that
    shines but does not burn.
Praised be hot vapors in earth's crust, for they force up
    mountains that explode as molten rock and cool, like
    love remembered.
Holy is the sun that strikes sea, for surely as water
    burns life and death are one. . . .

Grace Schulman, from "Blessed Is the Light"

   They lived long, and were faithful
   to the good in each other.
   They suffered as their faith required.

The Country of Marriage · *231*

Now their union is consummate
in earth, and the earth
is their communion. They enter
the serene gravity of the rain,
the hill's passage to the sea.
After long striving, perfect ease.

WENDELL BERRY,
"A Marriage, an Elegy"

May the wind be always at your back.
May the road rise up to meet you.
May the sun shine warm on your face,
The rains fall soft on your fields.
Until we meet again, may the Lord
Hold you in the hollow of his hand.

Irish blessing

God banish from your house
The fly, the roach, the mouse

That riots in the walls
Until the plaster falls;

Admonish from your door
The hypocrite and liar;

No shy, soft, tigrish fear
Permit upon your stair,

Nor agents of your doubt.
God drive them whistling out.

Let nothing touched with evil,
Let nothing that can shrivel

Heart's tenderest frond, intrude
Upon your still, deep blood.

Against the drip of night
God keep all windows tight,

Protect your mirrors from
Surprise, delirium,

Admit no trailing wind
Into your shuttered mind

To plume the lake of sleep
With dreams. If you must weep

God give you tears, but leave
Your secrecy to grieve,

And islands for your pride,
And love to nest in your side.

STANLEY KUNITZ, "Benediction"

Beautiful is thy rising upon the horizon of heaven, when the
    living Disk hangs vibrant.
Thou it is that shineth upon the Eastern horizon, and every
    land is filled with thy beauty.
It is thy beauty, the greatness, and thy splendor that cause
    praises to thee from every land when thy rays embrace
    their lands.
Thou compellest their love of thee, for though thou art far
    distant, yet do thy rays illumine the earth.
When thou takest thy rest in the Western Horizon, the land is
    in darkness, with thoughts of death. . . .

Day breaks at thy appearance upon the Horizon, when thou
givest light by means of the Disk by day; yea, darkness
flees when thou sendest forth thy beams . . .
Thou makest man to unite with woman, thou hast put a life-
giving seed into humankind, making live a child within the
womb of its mother . . .
If there is a chicken within the egg, thou givest it breath within
its shell, so that it lives. Thou makest it to unite all its
strength, so that it breaketh the egg, cometh forth from
the shell and calleth for its mother. . . . It walketh upon
its two feet.
Thou hast created the earth by thy mere wish when thou wast
the only one: all men and animals, all that goeth upon
their feet upon the earth, and all that fly on high . . .

AMENOPHIS IV (IKHNATON), hymn to the sun

Every day is a god, each day is a god, and
holiness holds forth in time. I worship each
god, I praise each day splintered down,
splintered down and wrapped in time like a
husk, a husk of many colors spreading, at dawn
fast over the mountains split.
    I wake in a god. I wake in arms holding my
quilt, holding me as best they can inside my
quilt.
    Someone is kissing me—already. I wake, I
cry, "Oh," I rise from the pillow. Why should
I open my eyes?
    I open my eyes. The god lifts from the water.
His head fills the bay. He is Puget Sound, the

Pacific; his breast rises from pastures; his
fingers are firs; islands slide wet down his
shoulders. Islands slip blue from his shoulders
and glide over the water, the empty, lighted
water like a stage.

Today's god rises, his long eyes flecked in
clouds. He flings his arms, spreading colors; he
arches, cupping sky in his belly; he vaults,
vaulting and spread, holding all and spread
on me like skin. . . .

The day is real. . . .

The day is real. . . . I stand and smooth the
quilt.
"Oh," I cry, "Oh!"

ANNIE DILLARD, from Holy the Firm

Libations! Libations!
To the protective spirits on high!
To the wandering spirits below!
To the spirits of the mountains,
To the spirits of the valleys,
To the spirits of the East,
To the spirits of the West,
To the spirits of the North,
To the spirits of the South,
To the bride and groom, together, libation!
May the spirits on high, as well as the spirits below, fill you
    with grace!

Divine helpers, come! Keep watch all night! Rather than see
the bridegroom so much as damage his toenail, may the good
spirits go ahead of him. May the bride not so much as damage

her fingernail! The good spirits will be their cushions so that not a hair of their heads shall be harmed.

And you, all you good wedding guests waiting in the shadows, come out into the light! May the light follow you!

African wedding benediction

... hand in hand, on the edge of the sand,

They danced by the light of the moon,
　　　The moon,
　　　The moon,
They danced by the light of the moon.

EDWARD LEAR, from "The Owl and the Pussycat"

Where will you and I sleep?
At the down-turned jagged rim of the sky, you and I will sleep.

Wintu tribe "Dream Song"

Suggested Readings for Various Members of the Wedding Party

The Bride

The Bridegroom

Father of the Bride

Mother of the Bride

Father of the Bridegroom

Mother of the Bridegroom

Parents, Brothers, Sisters, and Others of the
    Immediate Families

Close Friends

In addition to the above, many scriptural and liturgical passages throughout are appropriate for reading by all members of the wedding party. Officiants may wish to enlarge on their normal liturgical and scriptural readings with selections from "Eternal Vows in Sacred Space" and "Morning in Eternal Space."

Index

Credits

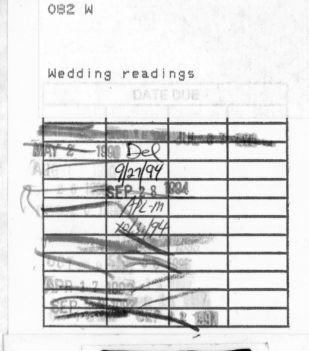